DATA ABSTRACTION IN PROGRAMMING LANGUAGES

INTERNATIONAL COMPUTER SCIENCE SERIES

Consulting editors **A D McGettrick** University of Strathclyde
J van Leeuwen University of Utrecht

OTHER TITLES IN THE SERIES

Programming in Ada (2nd Edn.) *J G P Barnes*

Computer Science Applied to Business Systems *M J R Shave and K N Bhaskar*

Software Engineering (2nd Edn.) *I Sommerville*

A Structured Approach to FORTRAN 77 Programming *T M R Ellis*

The Cambridge Distributed Computing System *R M Needham and A J Herbert*

An Introduction to Numerical Methods with Pascal *L V Atkinson and P J Harley*

The UNIX System *S R Bourne*

Handbook of Algorithms and Data Structures *G H Gonnet*

Office Automation: Concepts, Technologies and Issues *R A Hirschheim*

Microcomputers in Engineering and Science *J F Craine and G R Martin*

UNIX for Super-Users *E Foxley*

Software Specification Techniques *N Gehani and A D McGettrick* (eds.)

Data Communications for Programmers *M Purser*

Local Area Network Design *A Hopper, S Temple and R C Williamson*

Prolog Programming for Artificial Intelligence *I Bratko*

Modula-2: Discipline & Design *A H J Sale*

Introduction to Expert Systems *P Jackson*

Prolog *F Giannesinni* et al.

Programming Language Translation: A Practical Approach *P D Terry*

System Simulation: Programming Styles and Languages *W Kreutzer*

The UNIX System V Environment *S R Bourne*

DATA ABSTRACTION IN PROGRAMMING LANGUAGES

Judy Bishop

University of the Witwatersrand
Johannesburg

ADDISON-WESLEY
PUBLISHING
COMPANY

Wokingham, England · Reading, Massachusetts · Menlo Park, California
Don Mills, Ontario · Amsterdam · Sydney · Singapore · Tokyo
Madrid · Bogota · Santiago · San Juan

Cover graphic by kind permission of Apollo Computer Inc.
Typeset by Columns, Reading.
Printed in Great Britain by The Bath Press.

British Library Cataloguing in Publication Data
Bishop, J.M. (Judith Mary)
Data abstraction in programming languages.
–(International computer science series)
1. Programming languages (Electronic computers) 2. Electronic digital computers –Programming
I. Title II. Series
005.13 QA76.7

ISBN 0–201–14222–8

Library of Congress Cataloging in Publication Data
Bishop, J.M.
Data abstraction in programming languages.

(International computer science series)
Includes bibliographies and index.
1. Programming languages (Electronic computers)
2. Data structures (Computer science) I. Title.
II. Series.
QA76.7.B54 1986 005.13 86–3503
ISBN 0–20–114222–8

ABCDEF 89876

To Nigel

Acknowledgements

The publishers wish to thank the following for permission to reproduce material.

Association for Computing Machinery for Figs. 1.1, 1.2 and 1.3 adapted from SIGPLAN, 1981, Proceedings of the Workshop on Data Abstraction, Databases and Conceptual Modelling; and for Fig. 6.1 adapted from Andrews, G.R. and Schneider, F.B., 1983, 'Concepts and notations for concurrent programming', *Computing Surveys,* **15**.

Benjamin/Cummings Publishing Company, Inc., for the four Ada programming excerpts on pp.68–70 from Booch, G., 1983, *Software Engineering with Ada*.

John Wiley and Sons Limited for material in Chapter 4 which appeared originally in Barron, D.W. and Bishop, J.M., 1984, *Advanced Programming: A Practical Course*.

Preface

The period from the mid-1970s to the early 1980s was one of immense change and development in programming language design. The host of Pascal derivatives launched during this period – Alphard, CLU, Euclid, Mesa, Modula and Gypsy – all aspired to the three goals of reliability, understandability and verifiability. The achievement of these goals rested on the resolution of the new language issues of data abstraction and formal specification, but also led to a renewed look at accepted features such as data types, operators, loops, exceptions, input/output and modularity. The culmination of much of this research is embodied in the one language which is destined to become widely available – Ada.

This book is intended to show how the data abstraction revolution has affected the entire spectrum of language design, programming methodology and the way we think about programs. Specific objectives are:

- to introduce the *concept* of data abstraction;
- to investigate the *practical issues* in incorporating data abstraction into programming languages, both in-the-small and in-the-large;
- to show how *formal specification and verification* are intimately tied up with language design;
- to illustrate *current thoughts* on old language issues such as literals, loops, exceptions and input/output;
- to explore the application of abstraction to *concurrency*;
- to introduce the data abstraction facilities of *Ada*;
- to provide a thorough knowledge of the *literature* and the people at the forefront of language design.

The book represents a logical synthesis of the published literature for the last decade, and should serve as a starting point for further study in any one of the directions covered by each chapter. To make this easier to do, the references are grouped at the end of each chapter and I have endeavoured to refer only to those journals that are readily available, in particular the publications of the ACM and IEEE, both formal and informal. I have tried not to include references to old or hard-to-obtain papers, except when these have been reprinted, in which case both dates are given.

This book is the basis for a postgraduate course given annually since 1980 to computer science graduate students. The course consists of 20 lectures and is assessed by means of an examination and an essay; sample examination questions are given at the end of each chapter, and can be used by students to check their understanding of the preceding material. Examples of essay topics are given at the end and these are intended to encourage the student to study further in a particular area. My thanks are due to the students in my classes for their enthusiasm and interest in the subject, which have led to significant improvements in breadth and depth over the years. In particular I would like to acknowledge the work of Shaun Goodbrand whose class essay on exceptions is quoted in Chapter 7. Meryl Rahme and Richard Rodseth assisted me in testing the Ada programs and excerpts on the IBM NYU/ED (Version 1.1 April 1983) compiler.

A prerequisite for the course is a comparative study of programming languages, and knowledge of Pascal is assumed. Ada is used throughout the book but is introduced in Chapter 4; those without prior knowledge of Ada should read this first. Because there are so many languages mentioned in this book, I have chosen to stick to one style of typesetting for them, and to distinguish each extract with the language name. The exception is in Chapter 4 where Ada is assumed unless otherwise specified. Explanatory examples in a general language notation are given in plain roman type, undistinguished by any language name. For authenticity's sake, some of the complete Ada programs in Chapters 4, 5 and 6 are given as actual computer listings.

The book took shape while on sabbatical at the Computer Laboratory, University of Cambridge and I am very grateful for the friendly and stimulating atmosphere there and particularly for discussions with my office mate, Jim Mitchell. My colleagues at the University of the Witwatersrand have provided helpful comments and criticisms, and I thank them warmly. The editors of this series were very helpful in improving the structure of the book. I would like to thank especially Andrew McGettrick for the care he took in reading and commenting on the drafts.

Finally, I would like to thank the University of the Witwatersrand, the Council for Scientific and Industrial Research, and the Liberty Life Association for their financial assistance during the writing of this work.

J.M. Bishop
Johannesburg

Contents

Chapter 1 What is Data Abstraction

In this introductory chapter, we trace the history of data abstraction and identify the main areas of concern. The emphasis is on programming languages for the rest of the book, so here we take a brief look at similar movements in the fields of artificial intelligence and databases.

1.1 What is abstraction?

Abstraction can be defined as

> a general idea which concentrates on the essential qualities of something, rather than on concrete realizations or actual instances.
>
> [Ledgard and Taylor, 1977]

Christopher Strachey, a computing pioneer of the 1960s, explained abstraction by pointing out the difference between dates and numbers. Dates are discrete instances in time which may be compared, or checked for leap years, or otherwise manipulated in a small set of ways. If implemented on a computer, they may become numbers, but many of the operations on numbers, such as taking the square root or even addition, are quite meaningless for dates. Alternatively, dates may be represented as strings, but the same restrictions apply. The operations required depend on the abstraction, not on the qualities of the concrete representation.

Edsger Dijkstra [1972], another eminent computer scientist, once remarked that the amount of complexity the human mind can cope with is very much less than that embodied in the software he builds.

> The central problem in designing and implementing large software projects is therefore to reduce the complexity. One way to do this is through the process of abstraction.
>
> [Guttag, 1977]

By concentrating on the real qualities of the object being handled, the human's task is reduced in two ways. Firstly, one can think and work in the *familiar terminology* of the object, rather than coping with the jargon of the concrete implementation. For example, in dealing with dates, it is simpler to be able to ask 'does the date fall in a leap year' rather than 'is the year component of the date divisible by 4, etc.'. Secondly, one need not be concerned with the *actual details of implementation*, thus reducing both the amount of complexity and what must be known at any one time.

1.2 Program abstraction

A long-standing aid to abstraction is the subroutine. Subroutines separate

the abstract – *what* is being done

from

the concrete – *how* it is achieved

Viewed the other way, the subroutine is generally only concerned with

the method – *how* it achieves its goal

and not with

the reason – *why* it is being used

The languages of the sixties, particularly FORTRAN, possessed subroutines to reduce duplication of effort in writing programs that dealt with complex numerical methods or statistical techniques. Subroutines were grouped into libraries and some of these were widely available, such as NAG, IMSL and GPSS. Programmers could call up routines to invert matrices or perform a least-squares fit without having to know the details of how the algorithms worked. In fact, it was the existence of these libraries that caused FORTRAN to be preferred over newer languages like Pascal well into the seventies.

The reason why extensive Pascal libraries are not available is not only because of the effort involved; there is a fundamental problem with block-structured languages in accommodating externally compiled routines. In FORTRAN, all variables are local unless explicitly shared through COMMON lists or passed as parameters. Subroutines can be written and compiled as stand-alone entities, with any variables that must be seen by the user listed in the parameter list or a COMMON list. All the user has to do is set up the same lists and communication is established. Although simple in concept, this method is very hazardous in practice because there is no check on the two versions of the lists being compatible. A slight slip (e.g. two names interchanged) might go undetected, contributing to spurious results, which might well be accepted as correct.

Linking in subroutines in Pascal is equally hazardous in practice, and even more difficult in concept. Here, all variables are local to their own procedures and automatically shared by all inner procedures, but variables may not be shared across two unnested procedures except by parameter lists or the use of globals. Parameters are not always the most suitable vehicle for communication and in the case of large structures or frequent access they are certainly not the most efficient. Therefore, any variables to be shared have to be placed in the outermost block; that is, 'made global'. If a routine is to be compiled separately for a library, it needs a dummy main program where these shared variables are suitably declared. The program wishing to use the routine has to list the variables in exactly the same ordinal position in its globals, making it almost impossible to call two general routines from one program (since both would have variables competing for the first position in the global list). As with FORTRAN, there is no check that the communication through shared variables is correctly established, although Pascal does check that parameter lists are compatible.

Once this problem of separate compilation was identified, language designers started looking at how languages could provide shared variables in an easy and safe way. But the changes were not just connected with technicalities: at the same time, it was becoming obvious that something more than just subroutines were needed to crack the complexity problem and that attention should be directed towards the organization and protection of data.

1.3 Data abstraction

Throughout the post-Pascal period of the early seventies, language designers were busy exploring new avenues, the results of which were reported in three milestone conference proceedings:

- *Data: Abstraction, Definition and Structure*, March 1976 [SIGPLAN, 1976];
- *Language Design for Reliable Software*, March 1977 [SIGPLAN, 1977];
- *Data Abstraction, Databases and Conceptual Modelling*, June 1980 [SIGPLAN, 1981].

From these events, there emerged two ideas. The first was that a data type was not just a definition of a set of admissible values, but that the concept of type was intimately connected with the operations that were meaningful for its objects. The second idea was that the protection of data need not be left to the good faith of the programmer or the policing role of the operating system, but could actually be built into the language itself. Violations of protection would then be found at compile-time rather than left to be detected at run-time, with potentially more serious consequences.

A good deal of the impetus for both of these notions was the growing use of high level languages, particularly Pascal, in large systems software projects. As is now understood, large projects have problems of complexity which structured programming alone cannot cope with. What was needed was a revolution in programming methodology, and by the end of 1977 this movement had a name – *data abstraction*. Data abstraction enabled

- large systems to be broken down into smaller parts with logical *interfaces* based on the data being handled;

- these interfaces to stand alone as the *specification* of the system, with the actual implementation hidden and flexible;
- as much *protection* as is necessary to be placed on each interface.

Put succinctly, data abstraction aims to do for data what subroutines do for control flow; that is, to separate the 'what' from the 'how'. The central idea is that

> *a data type defines a set of valid values and the operations on these values.*

The focus has swung away from the algorithm and onto the data. Instead of having to arrange how to share variables, the variables become the central issue, and the operations that can be used with them are given there and then. Using a suitable notation, the type definition would be enlarged and look something like

type *name*
  definition
    scalar or structured type definition
  operations
    procedures and functions
  end *name;*

When variables of this type are declared, they may then use the operations. They may or may not also inherit other operations, such as comparison or arithmetic. By 1977, several languages were already providing this facility under a variety of names such as class, cluster, form, module and unit. All of these terms signify that the definition should be regarded as a whole entity, the type and its operations together.

In the ensuing years, these enlarged type definitions came to be known generally as *encapsulated data types* and then as *abstract data types*. By the time Ada was launched in 1979, abstract data types were the accepted starting point for languages and programs. It is no exaggeration to say that data abstraction has caused a new programming revolution – the 'old' revolution being, of course, structured programming. But the data abstraction movement stretches its net wider than just reducing complexity. It aims also to provide a framework for the verification of programs and a means of increasing man and machine efficiency in software production.

The purpose of this book is to look at how data abstraction is incorporated into programming languages, at the difficulties and problems this causes, and at the subsidiary issues that it raises in modern programming. The rest of this chapter looks at data abstraction from various viewpoints. Chapters 2 and then 7 survey the main practical issues. Chapter 3 covers the theoretical aspects – which are having a growing impact in practice. Chapter 4 introduces Ada and Chapter 5 looks at iteration, which is considered to be the crucial link between data structures and control structures. Chapter 6 investigates abstractions for concurrency and, finally, Chapter 8 looks ahead to the languages and issues of the future.

1.4 Data abstraction as modelling

The first general treatment of data abstraction occurred at the ACM SIGPLAN conference on *Data: Abstraction, Definition and Structure* [SIGPLAN, 1976] held in March 1976. It had been noted that in both the programming language area and the database area there had been a move towards more natural methods for handling large amounts of real data and the purpose of the conference was 'to promote and bring together these two relatively disjoint areas of research' [Ledgard and Taylor, 1977]. The conference was certainly successful in promoting the notion of data abstraction; so much so that it was followed by a workshop in June 1980 on the subject – *Data Abstraction, Databases and Conceptual Modelling* [SIGPLAN, 1981]. Here the two areas were joined by a third – artificial intelligence.

This workshop revealed that all three fields have interests in

- data types and how to define them,
- bases of knowledge,
- specifying abstractions,
- formal means for designing and analysing models,
- separation of abstract models from their representation.

The workshop ranged widely over the issues. Although a growing interchange of ideas was evident, the net result was the conclusion that the three approaches are distinct and must remain so. As Brodie and Zilles [1981] said in their summary:

> Although there appeared to be as many differences within the three areas as between them, attempts were made to distinguish artificial intelligence, database and programming languages. The distinction concerned
>
> - the nature of models,
> - modelling techniques,
> - purposes of models.

In order to crystallize the notion of data abstraction, we shall briefly survey the approaches taken by the three areas.

Artificial intelligence modelling

Artificial intelligence (AI) is concerned with modelling human thinking. As shown in Figure 1.1, evidence is gathered from the real world and used by both the model and the human mind to make predictions. The model is successful if its predictions coincide with those of the human. The modelling process is concerned with defining primitives and then devising search strategies that will discover the requisite combination of these primitives to achieve the goal. The resulting systems are usually designed for a particular set of problems or a small set of intended users. They are not usually intended for production use.

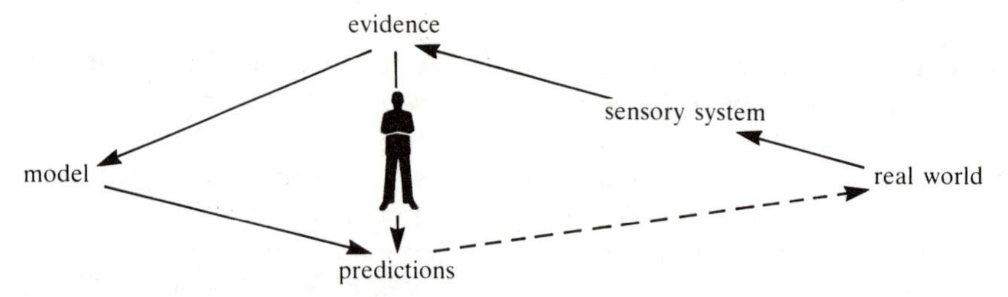

Figure 1.1 Artificial intelligence modelling by Ira Goldstein (in Brodie and Zilles [1981])

The above summary represents the 'power-oriented' approach to artificial intelligence modelling. Of growing importance is the work being done on *knowledge representation* – how to collect, define and handle expert knowledge in a computer system. Mylopolous [1981] surveyed the field at the workshop and felt that there was a definite similarity in the basic goals of knowledge representation research and that of semantic database models and programming specifications. In all three, the focus is on representation schemes for the formal description of 'a slice of reality', and such schemes must be as 'natural' as possible if they are to serve as a means of communication with the user. In artificial intelligence itself, the central issues are concerned with

- multiple use of facts by rules of inference and efficient access to the facts, even with incomplete matching information;
- incomplete knowledge, which may be added to throughout the lifetime of the system by the expert or the system's own experience;
- self-knowledge, such as the allowable configurations of facts or the strategies used by the system, and how this should be available to the user.

Mylopolous concludes that knowledge representation is maturing sufficiently to be a respectable subject to study. Good starting points are his paper, which includes a classification of representation schemes, and the special issue of *SIGART* on knowledge representation [SIGART, 1980].

Database modelling

Database modelling is concerned with capturing properties of interest to a set of real world applications.

As shown in Figure 1.2, database design attempts to extract application semantics from application programs and represent those properties in a central schema. The design proceeds in several steps, each modelling level having an associated validation technique. Traditional database modelling tools present fewer structures and operations than do AI and programming languages and the data is usually formatted and its meaning well understood. Database applications cover small- and large-scale productions. as well as naive and expert users.

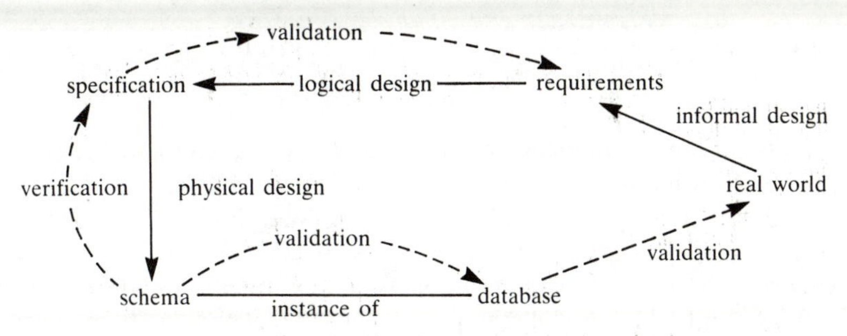

Figure 1.2 Database modelling (in Brodie and Zilles [1981])

In their survey paper at the workshop, McLeod and Smith [1981] gave their working definition of abstraction as

> a knowledge manipulation technique the essential purpose of which is to substitute a description of the essence of a concept for the concept itself.

The practical advantages of abstraction for the database community lie in being able to change the physical organization of a database without changing its logical structure, and to free the user from the burden of dealing with the physical storage and access details. In database terminology, this separation of the meaning of the data from its (presumably computer-oriented) representation is called *data independence*. Data independence is achieved by a model which works at several levels, known, according to ANSI/X3/SPARC [1975], by the general terms of

- *external schemas* – defining reorganizations of the data,
- *conceptual schemas* – specifying the meaning of the data,
- *physical design* – giving the storage structure and access methods.

Although all the representation detail has been abstracted away in the physical design, there still remains sufficient complexity in the logical structure to require further abstraction. Thus the classical database models (known according to their relationship topology as hierarchical, network or relational) are being extended to enable the data to be specified in a more user-understandable way. While removing many of the restrictions of these models, the new semantic database models provide facilities for imposing

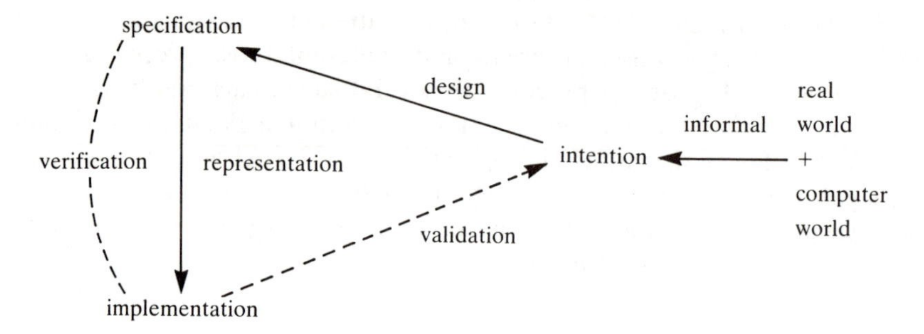

Figure 1.3 Programming language modelling (adapted from Mary Shaw in Brodie and Zilles [1981])

constraints on the relationships between data. The meaning of the data can then depend on its use and there can be multiple perspectives on the same data. (This theme of use dependency is being taken up by the programming language researchers as well.)

Clearly, therefore, abstraction plays a key role in modern database technology and the modelling process has reached a high level of standardization, while still advancing rapidly. Those interested in this area should start at McLeod and Smith's paper [1981] and the tutorial report that follows it.

Programming language modelling

Modelling in programming languages is concerned with the design of programs and the engineering of software systems.

The modelling process is confined to identifying the objects being dealt with, and the operations needed to manipulate them. As shown in Figure 1.3, the focus is on techniques that can achieve an exact specification of the intention and many formal verification and pragmatic validation tools are being developed. Unlike database modelling, the types are generally chosen by the programmer, not dictated by the application. The choice and method of specification are therefore more difficult as they are concerned with abstract notions. Many of the applications are man-made, for example compilers and operating systems, rather than real world. The behaviour of the model (in terms of resources and performance) is usually very important, since the models are most often intended for experts in production environments.

References

Brodie, M.L. and Zilles, S.N., 1981. 'Introduction to the Proceedings of the Workshop on Data Abstraction, Databases and Conceptual Modelling', *SIGPLAN*, **16(1)**, 2–4.

Dijkstra, E.W., 1972. 'Notes on structured programming'. In *Structured Programming*, New York, Academic Press.

Guttag, J., 1977. 'Abstract data types and the development of data structures', *CACM*, **20(6)**, 396–404.

Ledgard, H.F. and Taylor, R.W., 1977. 'Two views of data abstraction', *CACM*, **20(6)**, 382–384.

McLeod, D. and Smith, J.M., 1981. 'Abstraction in databases', *SIGPLAN*, **16(1)**, 19–25.

Mylopolous, J., 1981. 'An overview of knowledge representation', *SIGPLAN*, **16(1)**, 5–12.

SIGART, 1980. Special issue on knowledge representation, *SIGART*, No. 50, February 1980.

SIGPLAN, 1976. Conference on Data: Abstraction, Definition and Structure, *SIGPLAN*, **11**, special issue.

SIGPLAN, 1977. Conference on Language Design for Reliable Software, *SIGPLAN*, **12(3)** (also as *SIGOPS* **11(2)** and *SIGSOFT* **2(2)**).

SIGPLAN, 1981. Workshop on Data Abstraction, Databases and Conceptual Modelling, *SIGPLAN*, **16(1)** (also as *SIGMOD*, **11(2)** and *SIGART*, No. 74).

Chapter 2 Practical Issues in Data Abstraction

The practical issues in data abstraction can be summed up as how to define new data types and their operations and how to incorporate them in existing language structures. Across all languages, these points raise several side issues, which are discussed in this chapter.

2.1 What is a data type?

Historically, a data type was a name for one of a few predefined classes of values, such as integer, real or boolean, leading to the definition

a type is a set of values.

In the early languages that permitted it, such as COBOL and PL/1, new types were defined by specifying the representation of the values. For example, to set up a counter from 0 to 59 one would say

```
COBOL: COUNTER PIC 99.
PL/1:  COUNTER FIXED DECIMAL (2);
```

In both cases, the representation is given as two decimal digits – in effect permitting more than the desired range of values. In addition, operations available for any FIXED DECIMAL numbers, in PL/1, would be available for the counter, although presumably only +1, −1 and set-to-zero would be sensible.

As another example, consider a stack of integers, which would be defined

```
FORTRAN: INTEGER STACK (100), TOP
PL/1:    (STACK (50), TOP) FIXED BINARY;
```

There is no control over how the stack is accessed – TOP (or any variable) could be used to index into the array at any point. In short, any operation which is valid on the data type used to represent the abstract entity can be performed on it.

With Pascal, the position improves somewhat: the definition of new types depends on the abstract values desired, not on the means of representing them. So we have

Pascal: `TYPE counters = 0..59;`

which successfully excludes all the other values made available when variables of this type are implemented as, say, 16-bit integers. But Pascal still does not prevent nonsense operations on variables whose underlying representations are the same, in this case integer.

The next view, stated as early as 1973 by Morris [1973], was that types are not sets, but that

a type is a language mechanism to enforce authentication and security.

Here the focus is on the abstract level. The data type is defined by the abstract entities and operations which are encapsulated so that the only way to access or modify the entities is by the abstract operations. Hereafter, such definitions are referred to as *abstract data types*. Taking our example of a counter, we might set up a definition such as

```
TYPE counters
    DEFINITION
      integer range 0..59;
    OPERATIONS
      up (counters);
      down (counters);
      zero (counters);
      INHERITS '=', '<>', '<', '>';
END counters;
```

Thereafter we elaborate the operations in the implementation:

```
TYPE counters
    IMPLEMENTATION
      PROCEDURE up (VAR a : counters);
        begin
          if a = 59 then a := 0 else a := a+1;
        end; {up}
      PROCEDURE down (VAR a : counters);
        begin
          if a = 0 then a := 59 else a := a-1
        end; {down}
      PROCEDURE zero (VAR a : counters);
        begin
          a := 0;
        end; {zero}
END counters;
```

Note how restrictive the operations are: not only do they use + with an operand of 1 only, but the addition is circular.

At this stage, the revised concept of a type seems pretty clear cut, but the attendees at the 1980 workshop [SIGPLAN, 1981] found it not so. A special session was devoted to the question of 'What is a type?' and argument raged thick and furious, even within the programming language area alone. There seemed to be three distinguishable viewpoints which I shall call the pragmatic, the operational and the mathematical.

The pragmatic approach

Mary Shaw set out the pragmatic view. 'Types are not God-given and type is not a central point of the universe. More than anything else, the notion of type is a means of organizing information about programs. It forces the program author to deal with certain issues. It is a means of summarizing information about values common to a subset of the program's variables. It is a means of expressing the kinds of operations that may be permitted on those values. The motivation for type arises from a need for discipline in programming. It arises from the need to maintain the integrity of data, and in recent times it is used to reduce life-cycle costs of programs.'

In Shaw's view, therefore, we need types because we program, and the concept of type is directed to how we want our variables to look and be used. Put another way, the main use of abstract data types is to fill the gap between a set of values and operations that a user of a system would like to have and the set of values and operations provided by machine.

The operational approach

The operational view looked at how types were used and how they were embedded in the type system of a programming language. Central to this approach is that the operations can be generalized across several sets of values, all having common properties. In other words, the type, in this sense, is nothing more than a shorthand for writing out some long expressions that say, 'I am interested in objects that have this set of properties'. These properties can then be assumed for all uses of that object.

Not everyone was happy with this approach and it was variously described as being too rich and too difficult to implement in practice without excessive overheads.

The mathematical approach

Finally, the mathematical approach stated that

> *a data type is defined by a set of operations and a specification in some formal theory.*

If you have these two things, you can derive the set of objects. More formally,

> a data type is a many sorted algebra which is initial in at least one full subcategory of the category of all the many sorted algebras.
>
> [Goguen *et al.*, 1978]

Greiter [1982] in a critique of this view points out that

- it is not simple enough to be readily used,
- errors cannot be handled satisfactorily,
- a single algebra does not define a unique type.

Not discarding the view, he produces a simpler version of data algebras which claims to solve the above problems. When the need for a simpler view was queried, he responded [Greiter, 1983] with some home truths:

1. A definition for the notion of a data type is the more useful the less it depends on some special specification technique.
2. It is not very helpful to say that a specification for a data type is consistent if and only if it is Church Rosser: proving this property is nearly always a hard thing to do.

Those interested in the mathematical approach to data types will find Greiter's work refreshing, and can then work through the other key references [Goguen *et al.*, 1978; Guttag and Horning, 1978].

Despite the earnest debate, the consensus seemed that for practical purposes Mary Shaw's description was the best. In the light of it, we now discuss the other issues.

2.2 Type equivalence and type checking

For abstract data types to be incorporated securely into a program, there must be a means for identifying the type of an object and then checking that the operations requested are valid for that type. The simple approach is to require every type to have a name and then variables declared with the same type name are equivalent; any others are not. This would not permit sufficient flexibility in two areas:

1. Integer subranges may operate under many different names but such variables are frequently combined in expressions or passed as parameters.
2. Arrays with different bound ranges are likely candidates as actual parameters to the same operation.

There are many solutions to these problems, but Ada's seems to be the simplest and most consistent. If an integer-based variable of one declared type needs to be passed to an operation with a formal parameter of another integer-based type, then the actual parameter can be explicitly converted, as in

```
Ada:    TYPE index is range 1..max;
        TYPE cover is range 0..max+1;
        i : index;
        PROCEDURE increase (c : out cover);
     -- called by
        increase (cover (i));
```

(Subtypes are also useful in this context, as discussed in Chapter 5.) For an array, the operation need only define its formal array's bounds as unconstrained and then any actual array of the same type, but constrained with any bounds, will be acceptable. For example, if we have two vectors, one running from 0 to 10 and another from 1 to 100, then they can both be passed to procedure clear as follows:

```
Ada:    TYPE vector is array (integer range <>) of real;
        V10 : vector (0..10);
        V100 : vector (1..100);
        PROCEDURE clear (v : out vector);
     -- called by
        clear (V10);
        clear (V100);
```

Ada is very clear that anonymous types, i.e. those constructed in variable declarations, are distinct, even going as far as to say that variables declared in the same declaration with a type constructor are of different types, as in

```
Ada: a, b : array(1..10) of real;
```

The rationale is that this multiple declaration is textually equivalent to two single declarations, i.e.

```
Ada: a : array(1..10) of real;
     b : array(1..10) of real;
```

However, V10 and V100 above are of the *same* type – they are just differently constrained; an attempt to assign one to the other would result in a constraint error (hopefully at compile-time).

Thus Ada's type equivalence rests firmly on the name of a type, but with flexibility provided for by constraints and explicit conversions. To a large extent, this has defused the once heated debate as to whether types should have name equivalence or structural equivalence [Welsh *et al.*, 1977; Rowe, 1981]. Certainly, in the context of abstract data types, structural equivalence is difficult to justify. This is not to say that operations are strictly name-type bound, as there is plenty of scope for generalization via parameterized types, discussed in the next section.

2.3 Parameterized types

It was recognized early on that it would be very useful if some parts of an abstract data type could be parameterized. For example, our counter could act on any range of integers, so we would like to specify it as

```
TYPE counters (lower, upper);
  DEFINITION
    integer range lower.. upper;
  OPERATIONS
    up (counters);
    down (counters);
    zero (counters);
    INHERITS '=', '<>', '<', '>';
END counters;
```

Then objects of this type could be declared as

```
minute : counters (0, 59);
```

There would be a problem, though, when declaring

```
month : counters (1, 12);
```

because the operation *zero* as defined so far would assign an invalid value to *month*. This points out that *counters* was not sufficiently abstractly defined – we should have used the term *reset* instead of *zero* – and that the implementation needs to be generalized, with *lower* and *upper* being used instead of 0 and 59. In full, the revised *counters* type is:

```
TYPE counters (lower, upper);
  DEFINITION
    integer range lower..upper;
  OPERATIONS
    up (counters);
    down (counters);
    reset (counters);
    INHERITS '=', '<>', '<', '>';
  IMPLEMENTATION
    PROCEDURE up (VAR a : counters);
      begin
        if a = upper then a := lower else a := a+1;
      end; {up}
    PROCEDURE down (VAR a : counters);
      begin
```

```
        if a = lower then a := upper else a := a-1;
      end; {down}
    PROCEDURE reset (VAR a : counters);
      begin
        a := lower;
      end; {reset}
END counters;
```

This idea can be taken further to permit procedures to operate on parameters of any type, provided certain basic needs are defined. For example, when sorting an array, it is irrelevant what the subscripts or the elements are. The sorting process is only interested in the operations := and < being correctly defined. Suppose we define

```
PROCEDURE sort (var x : array [...] of ...);
```

where ... indicates that those portions of the type are not yet defined. With any declarations such as

```
a : array [n..m] of real;
pack : array [suit,1..13] of integer;
```

we should be able to call

```
sort(a) or sort(pack)
```

Effectively this means that *sort* will exist in several versions. The required version can be detected from the parameters in most cases; where this is not possible, ambiguity exists and the programmer will have to give more information. This problem is particularly acute with literals which may belong to more than one type. The issue is really one of subtypes, as illustrated by this example:

```
b : array [p..q] of real;
```

If *[p..q]* is contained in the range *[n..m]* then it is reasonable to suppose that

```
sort (b);
```

will use the same version of *sort* as that for *a*. Language designers are still giving this matter a great deal of thought and although Ada has semantics for subtypes the requirements of fully parameterized procedures are not yet realized.

Putting this idea into abstract data types means that there must be a proper notation for specifying at the start of the unit which parts are *generic*. These may include values, as we have already seen, or types or even procedures. Certainly, in the case of the sort example, it may be necessary for the 'less than' operation to be defined for each different version. Having so specified a generic unit, the next step is to *instantiate* it for each different version. Instantiation will most often produce an entirely new coded unit but, as we discussed above, it may be possible for very similar versions to share the same instantiation.

Keeping to our simple example, we may wish to have counters that work on characters or enumerated types or even a structure such as a date. Now we find that the +1 operation that was used in the implementation of *up* is not general enough. Using the usual term, we can replace it with *succ* which may be defined for integers and characters, but which we will have to define for dates. Similarly, *pred* will replace −1. The INHERITS part becomes more complicated: we assumed that we were inheriting these operations from the predefined ones, but if they are also to work on dates, then only = and <> can be used: < and > will have to be brought across from the operations defined in an abstract data type for dates. During instantiation, the compiler can search for these operations in a sensible order, looking first at the user's types and then at the predefined ones. The unit now becomes:

```
TYPE counters
    GENERIC
      type counters;
      var lower, upper : counters;
    DEFINITION
      range lower..upper;
    OPERATIONS
      up (counters);
      down (counters);
      reset (counters);
      INHERITS '=', '<>', '<', '>'
    IMPLEMENTATION
      PROCEDURE up (VAR a : counters);
        begin
          if a = upper then a := lower
                       else a := succ(a);
        end; {up}
      PROCEDURE down (VAR a : counters);
        begin
          if a = lower then a := upper
                       else a := pred(a);
        end; {down}
      PROCEDURE reset (VAR a : counters);
        begin
          a := lower;
        end; {reset}
END counters;
```

Suitable instantiations of this unit might be:

```
TYPE intcounter is counters (integer,0,59);
TYPE charcounter is counters (char,'A','Z');
TYPE monthcounter is counters (months, january, december);
TYPE datecounter is counters (dates);
```

and variables could be defined as before, i.e.

```
minutes : intcounter;
scale : charcounter (upper=>'G');
inseason: monthcounter (lower=>december,upper=>january);
year1983 : datecounter (lower=>(1,1,1983),upper=>(31,12,1983));
```

Here we have used the freedom to constrain separately the generic parameters at the time the variables are declared – a freedom that may not be available in all languages providing parameterized types. Clearly, the notation for the generic mechanisms must be very carefully thought out and their semantics well defined, but the above illustrates the intention simply enough.

A very important consideration with generic procedures is that the system must be able to check that the required operations are available for the type; in the sort example these would be := and <. This is relatively easy for an ordinary compiler to do. What it cannot do is to ensure that the operation actually performed by, say, < is the 'less than' relation which is expected. To check at this level of meaning would require the operations to be specified in a formal way, as discussed in Chapter 3.

2.4 Attributes, literals and aggregates

In the grand plan for data abstraction in a programming language, scant attention seems to be paid to the issues surrounding programming in-the-small; in other words, provision and notations for attributes, literals and aggregates. These features of a data type need to be powerful in order to support the full abstraction of the type from its concrete representation, which most often will be in numbers. At the same time, providing these facilities adds a new dimension to name resolution – a concept known as *overloading*.

Attributes

In their excellent paper on the practical issues facing language designers at the time, Gries and Gehani [1977] felt that one of the main points was that the domain of an array (i.e. its subscripts) should be a data type. An array *A* can be viewed as a function which maps the domain of subscript values onto the corresponding array elements.

```
  domain
    of      ———→  A  ———→      array elements
subscripts
```

The domain of A is a finite set of values of the subscript type, and can be expressed as *domain(A)* or, in modern parlance, *A'domain*. If A is defined as

```
VAR A : array [l..n] of integer;
```

then an index for A can be declared as

```
VAR i : A'domain;
```

This notation has all the advantages of abstraction – it says the essential bits (i is defined for the domain of A) while ignoring the actual type and range of that domain. In fact, i need not even be scalar. Consider the definition of a pack of cards

```
VAR pack : array [suits, 1..13] of integer;
    card : pack'domain;
```

Card is a record with two fields. Provided both fields are defined, *pack[card]* would be a valid subscripted reference to the array.

The purpose of these domain types is to be able to continue the abstraction into the iteration statement. Instead of having to say

```
for i := 1 to 10 do A[i] := 0;
```

we should be able to say

```
for i in A'domain do A[i] := 0;
```

and even

```
for card in pack'domain do pack[card] := 0;
```

In general, therefore, we can use the same notation to iterate over elements of any array, regardless of the number of dimensions and the type of the subscripts. Note, however, that no ordering of dimensions is implied: either field of *card* could vary faster during the iteration. If order is significant, the prefix *ordered* could be used and each dimension put in a separate loop:

```
for suit in ordered suits do
  for number in ordered 1..13 do pack[suit,number] := number;
```

Counting loops are not always suitable, though, and when a conditional loop needs a counter as well, additional attributes of the array are needed, viz. *A'min* and *A'max*. This gives:

```
i := A'min;
while (i <=A'max) and (A[i] <> 0) do
  i := i+1;
```

(assuming of course that AND is implemented by sequential conjunction!). Chapter 5 goes into loops in more detail.

The idea is, therefore, that we want to be able to access the essential properties of objects and to use these properties with standard names. Ada has provided this facility by defining useful accessible attributes for each class of type. The ones for arrays described above are called A'range, A'first and A'last and there are many more (see Chapter 4).

Literals

For an abstract data type to be complete, it should provide a notation for literals of the values it defines. The facilities that most languages offer for literals are meagre, being confined to the predefined integer and character sets and user-defined identifiers for enumerated values. One cannot usually take selective literals from another set, nor construct literals with any other lexical forms, such as being enclosed in angle brackets or colons. It can be argued that such freedoms would add substantially to the complexity of a program, rather than to its readability, and that the programmer should rather be guided into the correct way of using the simple facilities given. With this in mind, we look at what is possible and what is available.

Character sets

Every language has a predefined character set which is the one in which the language processor operates, and is usually that on the target machine. There are two problems which many languages simply ignore, i.e.

- unprintable characters,
- alternative character sets.

The unprintable or control characters have numeric values which when output cause some desired effect such as carriage return or form feed. In the older languages such as Pascal, one would set up a constant

Pascal: `CONST CR = 13;`

and convert this to character an output with

Pascal: `write(chr(CR));`

The great disadvantage of this method is that the programmer must remember all these numeric values, or know where to look them up. Ada has a rather elegant solution. The character type is defined in the standard package as an enumeration type, with the control characters given as 'invisible' identifiers, and the printable characters given in quotes. The order in which the elements are listed corresponds to the ASCII character set, and so the underlying value of each character will have the desired effect on an ASCII machine. Following this, a package called ASCII is defined, where all the characters that cannot be represented in quotes are declared as constants and initialized to their invisible names. These characters can then be referenced using the usual dot notation, e.g.

Ada: `put (ASCII.CR).`

This two-level approach to naming enables the predefined character set to be efficiently implemented, and yet still visible. To have an alternative character set, such as EBCDIC, we provide only one list of names and a mapping from them to ASCII, using the USE representation clause.

Numbers

In systems programming, plain decimal numbers are not usually adequate for representing the contents of memory or machine level instructions. Bases such as binary, octal and hexadecimal relate more visibly to the way words are divided up and it is desirable that values in these bases can be written directly in a program. Languages should provide a facility for indicating that a number is in another base. Ada's syntax is functionally correct, but not very pretty. The number is enclosed in hashes and preceded by the base.

Ada: `2#0000100011#    16#AF#    8#076#`

The usual convention for numbers from ten onwards being represented by A, B, etc., is used. The problem in finding a readable notation is that, for easy lexical analysis and conversion, the base must come first, whereas one normally writes the base last.

Enumerations

Enumerated values are now an accepted aid to readability, getting away as they do from the old ways of coding abstract entities with numbers. Ada has extended the original concept from Pascal and permits enumerated values to be identifiers or characters, which are considered to convey some meaning, but not numbers. Thus one can say

```
Ada: TYPE seasons is (spring, summer, autumn, winter);
     TYPE romans is ('I','V','X','L','C','D','M');
```

but not

```
Not Ada: TYPE romanvalues is (1, 5, 10, 50, 100, 500, 1000);
```

There is no indication in the literature that there is a practical problem associated with being able to select discrete integers to form a new type, and certainly in the example above or in

```
Not Ada: TYPE coins is (1, 2, 5, 10, 20, 25, 50, 100);
```

it is the natural thing to do. The implementation would follow exactly that for characters, entailing a mapping from the literals to the ordinal values defined by the positions and back again. In Ada, this mapping can be given explicitly for characters or identifiers, e.g.

```
Ada: FOR romans use (1, 5, 10, 50, 100, 500, 1000);
```

and could be used with the pos attribute to get the appropriate value for each letter. For example, romans'pos('X') would yield 10, not 2 as it would normally (the elements being numbered from zero).

Ada, as Pascal, does permit enumerated literals to be specified in more than one type and for subranges of them to be defined. For example, in the same name space as seasons and romans we could have:

```
Ada: TYPE operations is (divider, multiplier, differencer, summer);
     TYPE vowels is ('A','E','I','O','U');
     SUBTYPE sunny is new seasons range spring..autumn;
     SUBTYPE beforers is new romans ('I','X','C');
```

(There is more about these types in Chapter 4 on Ada.)

Apart from the omission of integers from enumerateds, the facilities Ada provides seem clear and powerful. However, there has been much discussion in the literature about the problems in applying scope and binding rules to them [Moffat, 1981; Harland and Gunn, 1982; Gladney, 1982]. The first problem is that enumerateds are in the same syntactic domain as variable identifiers, leading to potential name conflicts. Moffat [1981] gives the example of

```
Ada: TYPE colours is (red, white, blue);
     tone : colours;
     PROCEDURE try is
```

```
hue, red : integer;
...
hue := red;                    -- red is the integer variable
tone := colour(red);           -- red is the colour
...
```

and feels that Ada's solution – which is to add the type name to avoid ambiguity – is an example of *ad hoc* language design. It results in any unqualified name being accepted as a valid variable reference, whereas it could have been a syntax error in the use of a literal. Some of the more severe errors that can occur in Pascal in this context [Welsh *et al.*, 1977] are overcome in the latest Ada standard (MIL.STD 1815A, 1983) by forbidding anonymous types (except for arrays), so all enumerated types will have a name and any ambiguous values can be suitably qualified.

The second problem is that enumerated types follow static scoping rules, whereas other literals transcend scope. This enables a new enumerated type to occlude other literals at an outer scope, possibly making the program erroneous thereby. There have been various suggestions as to how to improve the lot of user-defined literals, all of them seeming to home in on two points:

1. Literals should be indicated (by a bar or quotes or whatever) so that they are not confused with other identifiers.
2. Literals should have universal scope as do integers, although both Harland and Gunn [1982] and Moffat [1981] advocate refinements which would keep the literal identifiers in their nearest needed block, but make the values themselves global. The latter is regarded as important when considering the correspondence of the literal's number across separately compiled modules.

Aggregates

Abstract data types are most often concerned with structures rather than scalar objects, as it is with structures that one really feels the need to define new operations. The provision of literals for structures is something that was only undertaken by the larger languages – Algol 68, PL/1 and now Ada. Nevertheless, it is an essential feature. We look here at the usual notations and at the problem that aggregates can pose for language designers.

The most popular way of writing an aggregate is to list all the components and enclose the list in parenthesis. The components may be listed

- *positionally*, i.e. in the order in which they appear in the structure's definition, or
- *by name*, i.e. the name of each component is given, followed by its value.

The first method seems suited to array elements and the second to records, but in fact both can be useful in either case. Examples from Ada would be

```
Ada: -- positional
        (25, december, 1983)                          -- for a record
        (31,28,31,30,31,30,31,31,30,31,30,31)         -- for an array

     -- by name
        (year=> 1983, month=> december, day=> 25)
        (sept | april | june | nov => 30, feb => 28, others => 31)
```

Ada permits several refinements which make its notation very powerful. For records, the two methods can be mixed, provided that the positional items all come first; several names of items can be listed for the same value, or ranges of subscripts can be specified; and there is an others clause which covers all items not named.

With such a bland syntax as a list in parenthesis, it is to be expected that there must be ways of recognizing aggregates and of deciding their type. The rules of Ada are sound in this regard. Firstly, an aggregate can be distinguished from an expression by either a comma, or if it has only one component (highly unlikely) its value must be given by name and the => can be detected. Secondly, the type of the aggregate is deduced solely from its context, and not from its components. This is an obvious decision, because a list of three integers, say, could be a literal for several different types. Thirdly, an aggregate must be complete, i.e. there must be a value for each component.

2.5 Input and output

Without a doubt, input/output (I/O) is the Cinderella of programming language design. There are no major treatises on how it should be done, the feeling being that any old thing will do. Yet real programs, from the very first 'add two numbers' of a novice to complex telecommunications systems of millions of lines, need to communicate with the outside world, and to do this they need facilities in the language. The history of programming is littered with languages that were used *despite* their lack of such facilities. FORTRAN is the classic example of a language that was almost feared because of the difficulty of coming to grips with its FORMATs. On the other hand, the phenomenal success of BASIC is due in a large way to its extremely simple and effective READ and PRINT statements.

Approaches to language features

There are two broad ways of handling input/output in a language, i.e.

- built-in statements,
- tacked-on procedures.

Most of the early languages used the first approach, providing read and write statements, or similar, with their own special syntax. In general, these statements were geared towards handling several items at a time, usually constituting a line of input or output. The advantage of such statements is that they are handy to use in most cases, and can be efficiently implemented. Since input/output is a relatively slow process, efficiency is an important consideration. The disadvantage of built-in statements is that they are confined to the facilities originally envisaged by the language designer, and cannot easily be extended. Examples of extensions that have been necessary are the handling of interactive processing and of more sophisticated file handling techniques. Moreover, these requirements often differ from machine to machine and providing for them can render languages, and hence programs, non-portable.

To ensure extensibility and portability, a language can simply adopt the procedure mechanism for all input/output facilities. This is the classic abstraction approach, pioneered by Algol 60, but it has its disadvantages. Firstly, in order to have some uniformity, a standard set of procedures must be agreed upon. Because these are then provided with every implementation, they are looked upon almost as built-in statements, with exactly the same problems mentioned above. However, they have the added disadvantage of being long-winded, in that each item must be passed, singly, to a procedure for processing. Pascal is the only language that mixes the two approaches, and in so doing gets around this particular objection. In Pascal, the read and write procedures may take any number of parameters of the types that can be handled, and in any order.

As an illustration, compare the output of a string and a number in various languages:

```
BASIC:     300  PRINT "The answer is ",X

FORTRAN:        WRITE(6,600) X
           600  FORMAT ("The answer is ",F8.4)

Pascal:    writeln('The answer is ', X:8:4);

Ada:       put("The answer is "); put(x,3,4); new_line;
```

The get-and-put approach is the one most new languages go for, but, apart from the inconvenience, it is very difficult to use in concurrent programs. Typically, one would want a process to output a whole message, which may be composed of several items. By supplying these to individual calls to put, one runs the risk of the process being interrupted in between puts, and a subsequent mess occurring in the printout. Exactly this problem was faced in the program given in Chapter 6, and the solution adopted was to use 'internal output' to construct the message as a string and then output it in one go. Thus instead of set_col to move across the page, we took a slice of an array filled with spaces, and instead of putting integers, we took their image attribute, and then catenated all the bits together. Compare the two:

```
Ada: set_col(column); put(name); put_line(" available");

     put_line (spaces(1..column) & names'image(name) & " available");
```

Generalizing input/output

Even without the provision of variable numbers of parameters, languages that adopt the procedural approach are faced with having to provide variable types of parameters for the same procedure. It is very awkward if there is a different procedure name to write each given type, let alone all the new ones that can be defined. Modula-2 has this approach. Ada's solution is to use generic packages for the given types, integer, float, fixed and enumerated, and to require the user to instantiate these for each distinct type. The statements to acquire input/output facilities in an ordinary program reading and writing integers and reals are:

```
Ada: PACKAGE int_io is new integer_io(integer);
     PACKAGE flo_io is new float_io(float);

     USE int_io, flo_io,
```

Clearly, it would be nice to be able to use Ada's abstraction facilities to hide such detail from the casual user. Such an attempt was made by Rahme [1984] who defined a package called Wits which included these instantiations as well as procedures to enable files to be named at run-time. However, this made int_io and flo_io local to Wits and hence not visible to users directly. To overcome this, all of the I/O procedures were mentioned again in Wits, and declared as renaming those of int_io and flo_io.

The moral of the story is that procedural input/output involves one in a lot of work, which may be daunting to the novice, irritating to the expert, and ultimately quite costly in both man and machine efficiency.

Semantic loopholes

Whether built-in statements or standard procedures are used, a language must give some guidance as to what can be done with input/output, and also how it is done. Once again, there seems to be no clear-cut solution to certain very simple problems. The classic case of a semantic loophole is in the definition of input in Pascal. Wirth's original design did not take account of interactive input, particularly the buffered interactive input used by terminals connected to mainframes. As a result, programs written with input from files could not run if the input was requested from a terminal and vice versa. It is evidence of the confusion that this can cause that no fewer than six articles were written on the subject in two years in SIGPLAN, culminating in the one by Perkins [1981]. The suggestions for eliminating the problem ranged from new styles of programming to redefining the get primitive, with arguments for and against. Despite this, Ada has not really addressed the problem either, and interactive input is not compatible with files.

Exercises

1. Discuss the two main issues in data abstraction identified by Gries and Gehani [1977] and examine the extent to which these ideals have been achieved in Ada, giving examples.
2. 'Name pollution is a necessary consequence of data abstraction.' Discuss this statement, with reference to Ada's attribute and package facilities.
3. Compare and contrast the statement and procedural approaches to input/output with special reference to their ease of use and their applicability to user-defined types. Illustrate your answer with examples.

References

Gladney, H.M., 1982. 'A note on enumerations', *SIGPLAN*, **17(12)**, 59–64.

Goguen, J.A., Thatcher, J.W. and Wagner, E.G., 1978. 'An initial algebra approach to the specification, correctness and implementation of abstract data types'. In *Current Trends in Programming Methodology*, edited by R. Yeh, New Jersey, Prentice-Hall, pp. 80–149.

Greiter, G., 1982. 'A data type theory', *SIGPLAN*, **17(5)**, 47–53.

Greiter, G., 1983. 'Comparing two definitions for the notion "data type" ', *SIGPLAN*, **18(7)**, 45–49.

Gries, D. and Gehani, N., 1977. 'Some ideas on data types in high-level languages', *CACM*, **20(6)**, 414–420.

Guttag, J., and Horning, J., 1978. 'The algebraic specification of abstract data types'. In *Programming Methodology*, edited by D. Gries, New York, Springer-Verlag, pp. 282–334.

Harland, D.M. and Gunn, H.I.E., 1982. 'Another look at enumerated types', *SIGPLAN*, **17(7)**, 62–71.

Moffat, D.V., 1981. 'Enumerations in Pascal, Ada and beyond', *SIGPLAN*, **16(2)**, 77–82.

Morris, J.H. Jr, 1973. 'Types are not sets'. In *Proceedings of the 1st ACM Symposium on Principles of Programming Languages, October 1973*.

Perkins, H., 1981. 'Lazy I/O is not the answer', *SIGPLAN*, **16(4)**, 81–88.

Rahme, M., 1984. *Ada as a Teaching Language*, Computer Science Honours Project, University of the Witwatersrand, South Africa.

Rowe, L.A., 1981. 'Data abstraction from a programming language viewpoint'. In [SIGPLAN, 1981], pp. 29–35.

SIGPLAN, 1981. Workshop on Data Abstraction, Databases and Conceptual Modelling, *SIGPLAN*, **16(1)** (also as *SIGMOD*, **11(2)** and *SIGART*, No. 74).

Welsh, J., Sneeringer, M.J. and Hoare, C.A.R., 1977. 'Ambiguities and insecurities in Pascal', *SPE*, **7(6)**, 685–696.

Chapter 3 Specification and Verification

In this chapter we introduce the twin notions of specifying the intended effect of a program before implementing it, and of verifying that the implementation does conform to the specification. Ideally, specification and verification should be central to all software development, but in reality the notations and methods have not progressed far enough to make this practical. Nevertheless, the research on these topics has had a profound influence on the way in which we program, and on the languages of today. Here we outline the main areas of research, emphasizing their effect on languages and the degree to which they are applicable in practice.

3.1 What are specifications?

The development of software can be divided into the following steps:

- requirements.
- specification,
- design,
- module coding and testing,
- system testing,
- maintenance.

The requirements come from the user and are in the form of a list of desirable features. The software engineer takes these, analyses them and conceptualizes a system that will perform accordingly. He then specifies what the system will do by giving a precise account of its proposed functions. Although the specification will quite naturally be arranged according to the inherent data groupings in the system, it is only in the design that an actual organization of the data and modules is given. From there, the implementation proceeds through coding and testing, and finally the system is accepted and is liable for maintenance and change. It is well known that this last phase can last a long time and be very costly.

The specification as described above is essentially a 'reply' to the user's requirements and must be understandable by him. For this reason, the natural choice for a notation is English. However, ordinary prose is notoriously ambiguous, and it is necessary to structure and order the specification in such a way that it can be checked for completeness, consistency and accuracy. The resulting document is often referred to as the Software Requirements Document or SRD, and an excellent discussion on the ways and means of obtaining it is given by Sommerville [1985].

From the SRD, design proceeds by the now accepted method of top-down decomposition into modules. Producing a logical and workable organization of the data and algorithms required by the solution is a creative process, but methodologies and guidelines can be followed to make this more reliable. Jones [1980] describes a rigorous approach which combines formal and informal methods. At the end of this phase, the modules have been decided upon and they have to be described in some way. These descriptions will be used by programmers to produce code, both for a module itself and for other modules that use it. We can now define what we mean by a specification:

> *A* **specification** *is a short and precise description of the data and functions of a module.*

Thus we are not dealing with specification in-the-large, i.e. systems, but with the level that has an impact on programming languages, i.e. modules. In this context, the user of the module is no longer a non-computer-oriented end-user, but should be seen as the person on the software team who requested the module, or as someone who may wish to make use of the module in another program.

The role of the specification

As illustrated in Figure 3.1, the specification is the link between the user and the implementor. Its role was explained in an early paper by Parnas [1972] in terms that are still relevant today:

1. The specification must provide to the intended user *all* the information that he will need to use the program correctly, *and nothing more.*
2. The specification must provide to the implementor *all* the information about the intended use that he needs to complete the program, *and no additional information*; in particular, no information about the structure of the calling program should be conveyed.
3. The specification must be sufficiently formal that it can conceivably be machine tested for consistency, completeness (in the sense of defining the outcome of all possible uses) and other desirable properties of a specification. . . . By this requirement we intend to rule out all natural language specifications.
4. The specification should discuss the program in the terms normally used by the user and implementor alike rather than some other area of discourse.

From the user's point of view, therefore, the specification is both a source of communication and an initiator of work. As such it must have

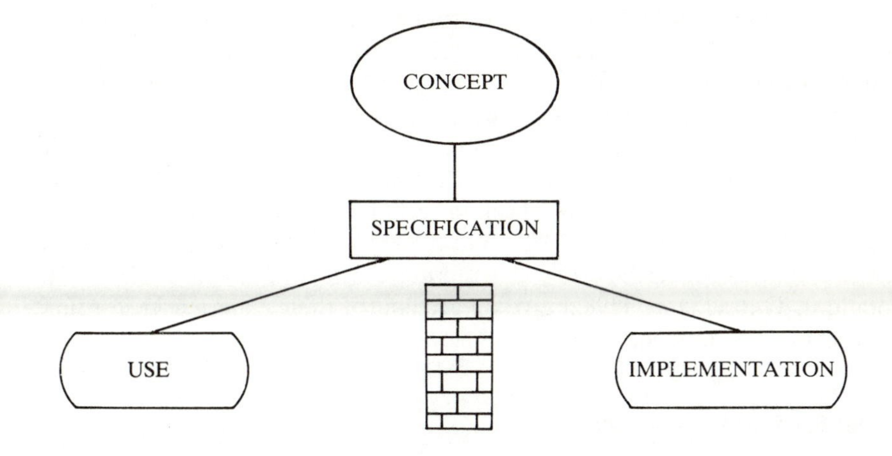

Figure 3.1 The role of a specification

certain desirable properties [Liskov and Zilles, 1975]. In the first instance, specifications must be *writable*, i.e. it must be possible to construct a specification without undue difficulty. In doing so, the writer must have confidence that he is accurately capturing the concept, and is not leaving anything out. Of equal importance is the requirement that the specification be *readable*. A person trained in using the notation should be able to reconstruct the concept that the specification is intending to describe. This is going to be much easier if the specification is short – in particular, it is usually said that the specification should be as least shorter than the final implementation! In this vein, Parnas's outline requires that the specification be *minimal* in that it should not describe anything other that the relevant properties of the concept. Especially, the specification should not make any preemptive assumptions about how the module will be implemented.

It would also be advantageous if the method of specification had a wide *range of applicability*, i.e. if the class of concepts that can be described in a straightforward way is large. This is not so for the methods of today, although this requirement is always borne in mind and commented on by those who propose specification techniques. Finally, we would like a specification to be *extensible*: a small change in the concept should result in only a small change in the specification.

Overriding all the properties given above is the requirement that the notation be sufficiently *formal* to be a basis for the process whereby the implementation may be verified to behave in accordance with the specification. This means that the description of the functions of the module will have to be given in mathematical terms, to coincide with a proof of a mathematical nature. Without such a formal specification, verification cannot proceed. Formality is both the justification and the downfall of specification techniques. As long as there is hope that verification will be a practical proposition in future, it is worth continuing to investigate the role of mathematics here. At the same time, the difficulty and strangeness of mathematical notation for most programmers makes it hard to even begin to introduce these techniques. Fair attempts have been made by Gries [1981], Wulf *et al.* [1981] and Jones [1980], and an outline of the role of specifications in verification is given in Section 3.4.

Specific comparisons of specification techniques are given in Liskov and Zilles [1975] and Cleaveland [1980], and the work of Marcotty *et al.* [1976] is also relevant in seeing how the above criteria can be evaluated for formal notations. Guttag *et al.* [1982] give an account of their experiences in using specifications in practice.

Benefits of specifications

From the viewpoint of the implementation, there are additional benefits which stem from the separation of what from how, namely

- flexibility,
- efficiency,
- protection.

As indicated in Figure 3.1, more than one implementation of a module may exist, provided they all conform to the specification. This gives the implementor the flexibility of making changes to the module, without the drawback of affecting his users. This property is especially important during the final phase of a project, i.e. maintenance.

Efficiency, too, is enhanced in that the language may only need the specification during the compilation of a program that uses a module; the implementation need only be drawn in at link-time. By the same token, if a new version of the implementation is developed, user programs only have to be relinked, not recompiled. It is important, though, to realize that full type checking is still preserved, because all the information necessary to check for valid uses of objects in a module is contained in the specification, which is indeed read by the compiler. Finally, protection is an important issue in large systems, and modules that define or manipulate sensitive data can hide this in an implementation.

Notations for specifications

The specification, therefore, is an encapsulation of the concept of a module, as seen by the user. Since it must be written down, the question is, in what notation? The specification is situated in the middle and needs to be understandable to the user, yet sufficiently precise as to be an unambiguous guide for the implementor. These are conflicting goals. To be unambiguous, a notation needs to be precise and formal, yet such properties make it very difficult to understand, except by experts. Nevertheless, progress has been made in this area. The development of formalisms – even languages – has proved an interesting and challenging task and there is some evidence of these being used in practical projects. The next two sections discuss the two approaches to formal specification.

In the literature, the standard examples for illustrating specifications are the stack and the symbol table. Although it has almost become hackneyed, we shall use the stack here, with the slight variation that it will be a stack of characters rather than integers. The reader may like to develop similar specifications for the counter type described in the previous chapter as an exercise.

3.2 Constructive specifications

The *constructive* approach to specifications involves finding some formal mathematical object – typically a set, list or sequence – whose behaviour is likely to reflect that of the abstract data type and to model on top of this the operations that we require. This is also known as the *operational* or *model* approach. The way in which the operations are described is usually in terms of assertions about the state of the data before and afterwards, a method first proposed by Hoare [1969]. In his notation,

$$\{P\}\ S\ \{Q\}$$

means 'If proposition P is true when control is at the beginning of statement S, then proposition Q is true when control is at the end of S'. P and Q are known as the *input and output assertions* or the *pre- and post-conditions*. In addition, there is usually an *invariant assertion* which holds for all operations. The conditions are formed using predicate logic, with the variables and values needed being listed initially.

To get an idea of this notation, Figure 3.2 gives a sample specification of a bounded stack with just the four operations: newstack, push, pop and top. The specification is modelled on the normal notion of array – not a very mathematical basis, but suitable for the purpose.

Except for the input/output value, x, the details of the state of each data item are given each time, even if that state has not changed. In the output assertions, the symbols S_0 or t_0 identify the variables as they were before the operation, as distinct from the new version. There are no error conditions given, as one would expect in a bounded stack, because the invariant assertion guarantees that t does not exceed the limits of the array. Obviously, the means by which this guarantee is carried out is part of the implementor's task.

Predicate logic is not very readable in its raw form and various improvements have been made to render the specification more acceptable to programmers. We shall look at one system where the specification is integrated into the language.

Specification *stack*
S is an array of n characters
t is an index into S
x is a character value

Invariant assertion
$0 <= t <= n$

Assertions
$\{true\}$ *newstack* $\{t = 0 \wedge S = empty\ array\}$
$\{t<n\}$ *push* $\{t=t_0+1 \wedge \forall j\ [1<=j<t \rightarrow S(j)=S(j_0)] \wedge S(t) = x\}$
$\{t>0\}$ *pop* $\{t=t_0-1 \wedge \forall j\ [1<=j<=t \rightarrow S(j)=S_0(j)]\}$
$\{t>0\}$ *top* $\{S=S_0 \wedge t=t_0 \wedge x=S(t)\}$

Figure 3.2 A constructive specification of a stack

Alphard forms

In the experimental language Alphard [Wulf *et al.*, 1976], a module is written as a *form* with three sections – the specification, representation and implementation. The specification section for a bounded stack is given in Figure 3.3.

This specification is modelled on the notion of a sequence, which is itself only informally defined. Apart from the functions leader, length and last

```
Alphard: FORM stack =
         BEGINFORM
         SPECIFICATIONS
           LET stack = <...xi...> WHERE xi is character;
           INVARIANT 0<=length(stack)<n;
           FUNCTION
             newstack(s:stack)
                 POST s=nullseq,
             push(s:stack; x:character)
                 PRE  length(s)<n
                 POST s = s'&x,
             pop (s:stack)
                 PRE  0<length(s)
                 POST s=leader(s'),
             top (s:stack) returns (x:character)
                 PRE  0<length(s)
                 POST x=last(s');
         REPRESENTATION...
```

Figure 3.3 An Alphard specification for a stack

which have the expected meanings, & is used for concatenations. Once again, S′ indicates the previous version of S in a post-condition.

Assessment

Let us look at how constructive specifications match up to the criteria discussed above. They are certainly formal, being based on formal logic, and given a good dose of 'syntactic sugar' they could be made to be quite readable and writable. One is encouraged to make the specification complete by giving output assertions for everything. Specifying each operation separately makes life easy for the implementor, as does the use of programming-like variables. The specifications are extensible, in that a modification in the definition of one operation does not usually affect others.

The disadvantages are quite serious, though. Firstly, using an underlying object may lead the user to conclude properties that are not intended or allowed. On the other hand, it may not always be possible or sufficiently straightforward to find a mathematical equivalent of the type to be modelled. Secondly, the very independence of the operations, which aids the implementor, works against the user in that it is not easy to convey the concept being modelled. In our example, if the names of the operations were changed to a, b, c and d, it would be quite hard to see that this module describes stack-like behaviour. The independence is illusionary in that the push and pop operations work hand-in-hand, as do pop and top.

In their favour, constructive specifications do put out some hope for practical programming. Apart from Alphard, a complete language system has been proposed by Claybrook [1982], which paper also includes useful examples and comparisons. Before leaving this section we consider one alternative notation.

An alternative

Cleaveland [1980] in a paper which compares three methods, comes out in favour of denotational semantics as a basis for what he calls *mathematical* specifications. Denotational semantics were first described by Christopher Strachey in 1971 [Stoy, 1977] and are now coming into the mainstream of computing along with the renewed interest in functional programming. Each operation is viewed as a function which transforms input values to output values and the specification defines what the function is, rather than how it goes about the transformation. Figure 3.4 gives the equivalent stack specification following Cleaveland's notation.

The symbolism is obscure, unless one is familiar with denotational semantics and lambda calculus. In brief, we have:

$[A \rightarrow B]$ is the set of all continuous functions from set A to set B;
$A \times B$ is the Cartesian product of A and B;

Specification *stack*
C = *set of all characters*
N = *set of all whole numbers*
$S = N \times [N \rightarrow C]$

$t,j \in N$
$s \in [N \rightarrow C]$
$x \in C$

functions
$newstack\ (\ ) = (0;\ \lambda j.\mathbf{void})$
$push\ (x,\ (t;s)) = (t{=}n \rightarrow (t;s),$
$\qquad (t{+}1;\ \lambda j.j{<=}t \rightarrow s(j),\ j{=}t{+}1 \rightarrow x))$
$pop\ ((t;s)) = (t{=}0 \rightarrow (t;s),$
$\qquad (t{-}1;\ \lambda j.j{<}t \rightarrow s(j),\ \mathbf{void}))$
$top\ ((t;s)) = (t{=}0 \rightarrow \mathbf{void},\ s(t))$

Figure 3.4 A mathematical specification of a stack

$(a;b)$	is a sequence of the elements a from set A and b from set B;
$a \rightarrow b,c$	means **if** a **then** b **else** c;
$f = \lambda x.y$	means $f(x){=}y$ (used for local functions where f is omitted);
void	indicates no value.

Thus, taking the pop function, we see that it maps a sequence of a number and a stack onto another number and stack. The right-hand side could be expressed as

if $t = 0$ **then** $(t;s)$
  else $(t{-}1;$ **for all** j
    if $j{<}t$ **then** $s(j)$ **else void**)

The type of the right-hand side is not always the same as the left, since top maps a $(t;s)$ onto a character, which is not in this case explicitly given the name x. It is quite difficult to establish the type of a function and this method could well borrow from the algebraic approach in specifying the type mappings initially.

The flavour of this specification is different from the other two. The outputs are given directly in terms of the inputs, instead of being embedded in the assertions. The grouping of the index and stack is useful, and conveys more about the structure than the other methods. The boundary conditions have to be explicitly catered for, so we have two cases depending on whether $t{=}n$ (in *push*) or $t{=}0$ (in *pop* and *top*). This means that the specification must state what the value of the mapping is in these cases. From the specification, we deduce that an attempt to *push* or *pop* over the edge of the stack results in a null operations, and a *top* on the empty stack returns **void**.

Cleaveland [1980] claims that this method is formal, easy to use, has a wide range of applicability and is easily extensible. Time will tell!

3.3 Definitional specifications

The definitional approach to specifications views a data type as an algebra for which certain axioms concerning the operations on the data hold. The operations themselves are just mappings between types. This approach is also know as *algebraic* or *axiomatic*. It is based on the work of Zilles [1975] and Goguen *et al.* [1978], with the chief promoter being Guttag, with several papers [Guttag, 1975, 1977; Guttag *et al.*, 1977, 1978]. Figure 3.5 gives the stack example.

---

specification *stack*
  s is a stack
  x is a character

operators
  newstack : → *stack*
  push : *stack* × *character* → *stack*
  pop : *stack* → *stack*
  top : *stack* → *character*
  size : *stack* → *integer*

axioms
  pop (newstack) = *newstack*
  pop (push(s,x)) = *s*
  top (push(s,x)) = *x*
  size (newstack) = *n*
  size (push(s,x)) = *size(s)+1*

restrictions
  top(newstack) *raises an* **underflow error**
  size(push(s,x)) >= *n* *raises an* **overflow error**

Figure 3.5 Definitional specification of a stack

The operator section defines the types of the mappings in a succinct way, but says nothing about their meaning. This is given by the axioms which express the relationships between the operators. A typical axiom takes a constructive operator such as push and applies the converse to it, i.e. pop, defining the result as the data structure one had originally. Note that the operators are purely functional and do not alter the parameters. This can make calling them somewhat verbose, as for example to push '*' onto a new stack and get it off again requires:

```
var ST : stack; ch : character;
  ST := newstack;
  ST := push(ST,'*');
  ch := top(ST);
  ST := pop(ST);
```

Guttag *et al.* [1977] point out that this is not very natural for programmers and suggest that there should be the possibility for expressing functions as procedures instead, with value-returning parameters.

Handling errors

Handling error cases in a definitional notation is very difficult. In Figure 3.5, we have used a restrictions section, much in the same way as the constructive methods use invariant assertions. Here the two cases of pushing over the top and taking the *top* of an empty stack are identified and declared as raising errors. The third boundary case, that of popping an empty stack, is covered by the very first axiom and results in a null operation.

This approach to handling errors is a satisfactory one, and one that is likely to work in the more difficult cases (such as determining the upper bound of a stack). It conforms to the '80-20' rule in that most cases are covered by the normal axioms, enabling them to be more effective in conveying the concept. Two other approaches have been discussed by Guttag *et al.* [1977]. The first is to impose an extra layer of functions on top of those required, which checks for errors before the other levels are called. The disadvantage of this is that the specification may become large and unwieldy and the normal and abnormal cases are intertwined. The second proposal is to make use of a universal **error** value and conditional expressions. Thus one could add to the axiom

top(*newstack*) = **error**

The case of the stack being full is trickier. We cannot simply add an axiom stating that

push(*s*,*x*) = **if** *size*(*s*) = **then error**

because the effect of this has to be propagated into all the axioms mentioning push. Thus we would need to redefine

pop(*push*(*s*,*x*)) = **if** *size*(*s*) < *n* **then** *s* **else error**
top(*push*(*s*,*i*)) = **if** *size*(*s*) < *n* **then** *x* **else error**

which becomes cumbersome and reduces the readability considerably. Although axioms phrased in this way will be easy to implement, Guttag suggests that the implementation of restrictions is just as easy for a reasonably clever compiler. Both the **error** value approach and the restriction section are used in the literature.

Hidden operations

In order to handle a bounded stack (not often done in the literature) the extra operation, *size*, had to be introduced. Extra operations are often necessary, particularly if one wishes to scan through a data structure and have the notion of a current record, as discussed in examples by Cleaveland and also by Majster [1977]. During scanning, the data structure is viewed as consisting of two halves, with the current record being the last of the first part. Suppose, for illustration, we wish to add to the stack example the following operators:

$$\begin{array}{ll} advance & : stack \rightarrow stack \\ back & : stack \rightarrow stack \\ insert & : stack \times character \rightarrow stack \end{array}$$

where *insert* will put the character in the stack at the current position. We would add the mapping operator

$$M \quad : stack \times stack \rightarrow stack$$

which splits the stack into the parts, left and right, with the current position being at the end of left, and declare the axioms

$$\begin{array}{l} advance\ (M(left,insert(right,x))) = M(insert(left,x),right); \\ advance\ (M(left,newstack)) = M(left,\ newstack) \\ back\ (M(insert(left,x)right) = M(left,insert(right,x)) \\ back\ (M(newstack,right)) = M(newstack,right) \\ insert\ (M(left,right),x) = M(insert(left,x),right) \end{array}$$

These axioms are recursive, and will need additional axioms that give the stopping conditions. To see how they work, suppose we have seven characters in the file and wish to add one after the current position, which is 3. The left part is given by

$$(insert(insert(insert(newstack,c1),c2),c3))$$

and the right part by

$$(insert(insert(insert(insert(newstack,c7),c6),c5),c4))$$

so that we have

insert (*M*(*left*,*right*),*x*)
= *M*(*insert*(*insert*(*insert*(*insert*(*newstack*,*c1*),*c2*),*c3*),*x*),
M(*insert*(*insert*(*insert*(*insert*(*newstack*,*c7*),*c6*),*c5*),*c4*)))

The expression *M*(*left*,*newstack*) means the end of the stack. Using this, we can eliminate the *size* operator, which did not quite fit in with the others, and rewrite the restriction concerned with pushing over the limit as

push(*M*(*left*,*newstack*),*x*) raises an **error**
insert(*M*(*left*,*newstack*,*x*)) raises an **error**.

Assessment

Definitional specifications are certainly formal and they have been used in program verification. They are minimal, and do not preempt any representation decisions, as can be seen from the absence of any top or current points in the example. A series of axioms views the operators as forming trees, which limits their applicability to data types that can be represented as expressions. Although practice makes writing them easier, it is hard to know when the axioms are complete, and automatic prompting methods may help here.

To gain more idea about the applicability of definitional specifications to data types, one can read Guttag's work, as well as the two specifications of a Pascal file type [Laut, 1983] and a Pascal compiler [Despeyroux, 1983]. In terms of their use in practice, both Guttag *et al.* [1978] and Moitra [1982] describe implementations that take the axioms and produce the real operators. Of particular interest is the work of Gannon *et al.* [1981] whose DAISTS system employs user-supplied test data to investigate the consistency of a definitional specification with its implementation.

3.4 Progress with verification

Program verification was propounded in the late sixties and has been a thorny issue in computer science ever since. It is not within the scope of this book to give a tutorial on how it is done. Instead we examine what verification could achieve and how it affects data abstraction in programming languages.

The role of verification

Verification is the term used for 'proving a program correct' by formal means. Obviously the correctness of a program is very important. There are essentially three ways of establishing correctness:

1. look and see,
2. test exhaustively,
3. express the program formally and apply a proof.

The first method is very widely used but it has the disadvantage that the 'proof' is not visible or transferable or very reliable, and therefore not very convincing! Testing is the next most popular option, but the difficulty is in devising tests that are exhaustive. One of the most encouraging real applications of testing is the Compiler Validation Suites which have been devised for Pascal [Wichmann and Ciechanowicz, 1983] and Ada [Goodenough, 1980]. These have gained such acceptance in the community that all Ada compilers that are to be used by the Department of Defense (USA) have to pass a validation test.

The third method involves two stages. Initially, the meaning of the program must be expressed formally, and we have seen how this is done using specifications. Then the behaviour of the implementation of the program written in a programming language must be proven by some formal means to conform to the specification. The formality of both stages is not in itself daunting to ordinary programmers – possibly the abstract symbolic notations used have a lot to do with making verification unpopular. Perhaps work can be done in making these notations more readable, in the same way that programs are now considered readable without comments, or perhaps what is needed is a 'mathematical revolution' akin to the structured programming and data abstraction movements. Whatever progress is made in making verification more acceptable, we must realize that it is not meant to replace the other two approaches to correctness. Two of the chief proponents of formal verification advocate that a balance is necessary. Dijkstra [1976] writes:

> I have dealt with the examples in different degrees of formality. This variation was intended, as I would not like to give my readers the impression that a certain, fixed degree of formality is the 'right one'. I prefer to view formal methods as tools, the use of which might be helpful.

and Gries [1981] states the principle:

> Use theory to provide insight; use common sense and intuition where it is suitable, but fall back on the formal theory for support when difficulties and complexities arise.

(I am grateful to Thompson [1983] for identifying these quotations.)

Verification in-the-small

At the statement level, the meaning of a program is couched in terms of assertions about the state of the variables involved. Assertions typically are written at the beginning and end of blocks and loops. The proof then proceeds by either back substitution – where the assertion is applied back into the program statements until a prior assertion is reached and evaluated

– or by symbolic execution, which works the other way round. In both cases, the result of the proof is simply true or false – or perhaps nothing if the program does not terminate. Proving termination is therefore an important aspect. McGettrick [1982] is an excellent, practical text covering a full range of programs verified using Ada.

It seems natural that a language in which programs to be verified are written should provide for these assertions, and both Alphard (see Figure 3.3) and Euclid [Lampson *et al.*, 1981] do so. Every module allows initial, final and invariant assertions to be made, and an assert statement can be placed anywhere. The effect of the assertions is that the compiler must at that point evaluate the expression, or generate a run-time check to do so. An example of a Euclid function for finding the maximum value in an array is:

```
Euclid: FUNCTION FindMax (a : DataArraySegment(PARAMETER,
                                                PARAMETER));
          RETURNS index : SignedInt =
          POST {k in a.m..a.n. → a(index) >= a(k))}
          BEGIN
            index := a.m.;
            for i in a.m.+1 to a.n. loop
              assert {k in a.m..i−1 → a(index) >= a(k)}
              if a(i) > a(index) then index := i end if;
            end loop;
          END FindMax
```

An interesting outcome of the verification process is *program synthesis*. Using theorem-proving techniques such as transformation rules, unification and mathematical deduction, a program can be systematically constructed from its specification. The prime paper in this area is Manna and Waldinger [1980] which provides a tutorial view of program synthesis with ample examples. In Dershowitz and Manna [1977] it is shown how these techniques can be used to transform one program to another that uses the same principles in order to achieve a new or modified specification. Here is the forefront of automatic programming.

Verification in-the-large

The constructs available in languages today allow a programmer to isolate an abstraction, specifying its behaviour publicly, while hiding knowledge of its implementation. The verification of such an abstraction consists of showing that its implementation behaves in accordance with its public specification. Once this has been done, the abstraction can be used with confidence in constructing other programs and the verification of these employs only the public specification. Thus we separate the proof of the use of an abstraction from the proof of its implementation.

Verification in the Alphard system has been well documented by Wulf *et al.* [1976] and one of the points they raise is important. When dealing with abstract data types, we must at some point be concerned with the representation of the objects. To preserve the advantages of the abstraction, we wish to delay fixing the representation as long as possible. In Alphard this is achieved by describing the abstract objects and operations, then characterizing the concrete implementation of them, and linking the two by means of a function *rep* which must be able to map any abstract object into a (not necessarily distinct) concrete one. The proof method works in stages, ensuring that the representation, the concrete implementation and the relationship between them holds.

It is interesting to see the effect of this separation of abstract, concrete and representation on Ada. In Ada, the private types enable one to hide the representation of objects. However, the Ada compiler needs to know this representation in order to generate code for the using package. The private part is therefore in the specification section, rather than in the implementation where it belongs.

The effect on language design

The effect of the prospect of verification on programming language design has been two-fold. There has been a general improvement in the simplicity and overall structure of languages, and certain particular features have definitely become unpopular. These are side-effects, aliasing and procedure parameters.

1. *Side-effects*. Functions that permit side-effects make verification difficult because the result of the function cannot be asserted to be the same for the same input. For this reason, languages such as Euclid and Turing [Holt and Cordy, 1983] forbid them. Specifically, one cannot have value returning parameters and, more seriously, one cannot put debugging write statements in functions during development.
2. *Aliasing*. This is the term given to the process whereby a variable can have its value altered by reference to more than one name. For example, in

   ```
   PROCEDURE x (a,b : out item);
   ```

   called with

   ```
   x (n,n)
   ```

   there are three ways of accessing *n* from within *x* – via *a*, *b* and the global name *n*. Euclid and Turing and, to a lesser extent, Ada, forbid aliasing and go to great pains to detect it [Cordy, 1984].
3. *Procedure parameters*. Procedure parameters, and the variants of them, namely procedure variables and call-by-name parameters, cause execution to be performed outside the environment of the substantive procedure. Once again, this makes verification very difficult. At the same time, the lack of procedure parameters presents several practical problems in realizing abstract data types to the full. A full explanation for the lack of a

procedure parameter mechanism in Ada is given in Brosgol [1984], where he cites a horror of aliasing, concern for run-time efficiency and avoiding of complexity as reasons. His suggestion that generics are adequate to supply the required variation is put to the test in Chapter 5.

It is interesting to compare the partial demise of these features with the almost complete collapse of the GOTO statement. Since Dijkstra considered it harmful [Dijkstra, 1968], the GOTO has gradually fallen into complete disuse, despite a prolonged and spirited defence begun by Rice [1968] and highlighted by Knuth [1974]. Modern languages still have GOTOs in their syntax, but most programmers are not taught how to use them. The rationale is that GOTOs are unnecessary and that all desired control transfers can *just as easily* be achieved using proper control constructs. This is not so for the three features mentioned above, and more research into obtaining the desired effects, while not prejudicing verification, is required.

Exercises

1. Discuss the importance and relevance of definitional specifications in the construction and verification of programs. Discuss either Guttag's algebraic method or the logical approach used in Alphard, illustrating your answer with examples.

2. Abstraction can be defined as 'a general idea which concentrates on the essential qualities of something, rather than on concrete realizations or actual instances'. Discuss this statement with reference to the design of programming languages, and the need for formal specifications of programs which are to be verified.

3. Describe the use of the *specification*, the *representation* and the *implementation* of an Alphard form to implement abstract data types.

4. 'Use common sense and intuition where it is suitable, but fall back on the formal theory for suport when difficulties and complexities arise.' [Gries, 1982].

Discuss how formal specification and verification techniques can be said to support program design. Mention the problems associated with current techniques. Use short examples to illustrate your answer.

References

Brosgol, B., 1984. 'Ada implementation notes – passing subprograms as parameters', *Ada Letters*, **III(6)**, 118–120.

Claybrook, B.G., 1982. 'A specification method for specifying data and procedural abstractions', *IEEE-SE*, **8(5)**, 449–459.

Cleaveland, J.C., 1980. 'Mathematical specifications', *SIGPLAN*, **15(12)**, 31–42.

Cordy, J.R., 1984. 'The compile-time detection of aliasing in Euclid programs', *SPE*, **8(8)**, 755–768.

Dershowitz, N. and Manna, Z., 1977. 'The evolution of programs: automatic program modification', *IEEE-SE*, **3(6)**, 377–385.

Despeyroux, J., 1983. 'An algebraic specification of a Pascal compiler', *SIGPLAN*, **18(12)**, 34–48.

Dijkstra, E.W., 1968. 'Go to statement considered harmful', *CACM*, **1(3)**, 147–148 (reprinted, 1983, in *CACM*, **26(1)**, 73–74).

Dijkstra, E.W., 1976. *A Discipline of Programming*, New Jersey, Prentice-Hall.

Gannon, J., McMullin, P. and Hamlet, R., 1981. 'Data-abstraction, implementation and testing', *TOPLAS*, **3(3)**, 211–223.

Goguen, J.A., Thatcher, J.W. and Wagner, E.G., 1978. 'An initial algebra approach to the specification, correctness and implementation of abstract data types'. In *Current Trends in Programming Methodology*, edited by R. Yeh, New Jersey, Prentice-hall, pp. 80–149.

Goodenough, J.B., 1980. 'The Ada compiler validation capability', Proceedings of the ACM-SIGPLAN Conference on the Ada Programming Language. In *SIGPLAN*, **15(11)**, 1–8.

Gries, D., 1981. *The Science of Programming*, New York, Springer-Verlag.

Guttag, J.V., 1975. *The Specification and Application to Programming of Abstract Data Types*, Ph.D. thesis, University of Toronto, available as Computer System Research Report CSRG–59.

Guttag, J.V., 1977. 'Abstract data types and the development of data structures', *CACM*, **20(6)**, 396–404.

Guttag, J.V., Horowitz, E. and Musser, D.R., 1977. 'Some extensions to algebraic specifications'. In Proceedings of LDRS, *SIGPLAN*, **12(3)**, 63–67.

Guttag, J.V., Horowitz, E. and Musser, D.R., 1978. 'Abstract data types and software validation', *CACM*, **21(12)**, 1048–1064.

Guttag, J., Horning, J. and Wing, J., 1982. 'Some notes on putting formal specifications to productive use', *Science of Computer Programming*, **2**, 53–68.

Hoare, C.A.R., 1969. 'An axiomatic basis for computer programming', *CACM*, **12(10)**, 576–580 (reprinted, 1983, in *CACM*, **26(1)**, 53–56).

Holt, R.C. and Cordy, J.R., 1983. *The Turing Language Report*, Technical report CSRG–153, Computer Systems Research Institute, University of Toronto.

Jones, C.B., 1980. *Software Development – a Rigorous Approach*, London, Prentice-Hall.

Knuth, D.E., 1974. 'Structured programming with go to statements', *Computing Surveys*, **6(4)**, 261–302.

Lampson, B.W., Horning, J.J., London, R.W., Mitchell, J.G. and Popek, G.J., 1981. *Report on the Programming Language Euclid*, XEROX PARC research report 1981 (after an earlier version, 1977, in *SIGPLAN*, **12(2)**).

Laut, A., 1983. 'An algebraic specification of Pascal's file type', *SIGPLAN*, **18(4)**, 66–68.

Liskov, B.H. and Zilles, S.N., 1975. 'Specification techniques for data abstractions', *IEEE-SE*, **1(1)**, 7–19.

Majster, M.E., 1977. 'Limits of the "algebraic" specification of abstract data types', *SIGPLAN*, **12(10)**, 37–42.

Manna, Z. and Waldinger, R., 1980. 'A deductive approach to program synthesis', *TOPLAS*, **2(1)**, 90–121.

Marcotty, M., Ledgard, H.F. and Bochmann, G.V., 1976. 'A sampler of formal definitions', *Computing Surveys*, **8(2)**, 191–276.

McGettrick, A.D., 1982. *Program Verification Using Ada*, Cambridge, Cambridge University Press.

Moitra, A., 1982. 'Direct implementation of algebraic specification of abstract data types', *IEEE-SE*, **8(1)**, 12–20.

Parnas, D.L., 1972. 'A technique for software module specification with examples', *CACM*, **15(5)**, 330–336 (reprinted, 1983, in *CACM*, **26(1)**, 75–78).

Rice, J.R., 1968. 'The go to statement reconsidered', *CACM*, **13(8)**, 538 (reprinted, 1983, in *CACM*, **26(1)**, 74).

Sommerville, I., 1985. *Software Engineering*, 2nd edn, Wokingham, Addison-Wesley.

Stoy, J.E., 1977. *Denotational Semantics: The Scott-Strachey Approach to Programming Language Theory*, Boston, Mass., MIT Press.

Thompson, J.R., 1983. 'The use and abuse of formal proofs', *SIGPLAN*, **18(7)**, 75–79.

Wichmann, B.A. and Ciechanowicz, Z.J., 1983. *Pascal Compiler Validation*, Chichester, John Wiley.

Wulf, W.A., London, R.L. and Shaw, M., 1976. 'An introduction to the construction and verification of Alphard programs', *IEEE-SE*, **2(4)**, 253–265.

Wulf, W.A., Shaw, M., Hilfinger, P.N. and Flon, L., 1981. *Fundamental Structures of Computer Science*, New York, Addison-Wesley.

Zilles, S.N., 1975. *Data Algebra: A Specification Technique for Data Structures*, Ph.D. dissertation, Project MAC, MIT, Cambridge USA.

Chapter 4 **Data Abstraction in Ada**

Ada is now at the interim stage of development when books, courses and compilers are becoming available and anyone can learn the language. Until more experience is gained, though, it is difficult to assess exactly how one would program using the full power of Ada. The small copy-book examples that help one to learn do not assist in the larger issues of whether Ada does provide for increased productivity and reliability. The purpose of this chapter is to examine Ada in the context of its associated languages, for which experience does exist, and to emphasize the features that will make a difference to programming practice in the next decade.

4.1 The background to Ada

Much has been written on the history of Ada and most books, articles and courses start off with the political and sociological background to the Ada project [Barnes, 1980; Department of Defense, 1983; Ichbiah *et al.*, 1979]. Of more interest now is its technological background – what languages provided the foundation for its design, and what were the forces that influenced its final definition.

Pascal and the early seventies

The development of Ada can be seen against the backdrop of the whole language research effort of the seventies, which began with Pascal in 1971. Pascal was born out of frustration with the mammoth languages of the late sixties, namely Algol 68 and PL/1 [Wirth, 1971, 1976]. Wirth took as his design goals

- simplicity
- efficiency
- programming insight

and in all three his language achieved full marks. While simplicity and efficiency rocketed Pascal to the position where it is now available on a wider range of machines than any other language, it was the third goal – programming insight – that has made Pascal the accepted starting point for language design since.

What, then, were the features of Pascal that made it interesting? It had a clear, clean *procedure structure*, which was basically that of Algol 60 but with the rough edges smoothed over. It had the control structures of the *structured programming* revolution firmly embedded in its syntax, a move which contributed to the natural extinction of the GOTO statement. And, finally, it captured the concept of *data types* in such a simple yet powerful way that they could be used effectively in practice and yet still provide food for research to this day [Moffat, 1981]. In contrast, Algol 68 types were very interesting from the theoretical point of view, but painfully difficult to grasp in practice, and PL/1's data structures did the job but left researchers stone cold.

After Pascal – the late seventies

Pascal, therefore, was a solid foundation for research, while at the same time becoming a *de facto* standard for teaching and one of the first high level languages used for systems programming. Throughout the next five years, from 1971 to 1976, language designers were busy exploring new avenues, the results of which were reported in the two milestone conferences mentioned earlier (SIGPLAN, 1976, 1977]. By 1977 there were many languages supporting some kind of data abstraction facilities, each of them having a small but keen following. Some of these were Euclid [Lampson *et al.*, 1977], Modula [Wirth, 1977], Gypsy [Ambler *et al.*, 1977], Alphard [Shaw *et al.*, 1976], CLU [Liskov *et al.*, 1977], Sue [Clark and Horning, 1971] and LIS [Ichbiah *et al.*, 1974].

The emergence of Ada

Out of this experience, Ada was born. The structure and design of these languages were examined and refined for the definition of Preliminary Ada in 1979 [Ichbiah *et al.*, 1979]. Data abstraction became the cornerstone of the language, governing the underlying structure which, true to its antecedents, looks dominantly like Pascal.

There were also powerful influences on Ada from two other sources. Data abstraction was the input of the systems programmers, but two other groups of prospective users needed additional consideration, namely the scientific and real-time communities. For the scientists, the capability to specify and control numerical data was built in, chiefly by Brian Wichmann, and was based on many years of experience of machine-independent numerical packages. For process control, Ada has a rich high level real-time capability developed mainly by John Barnes who had been involved with real-time languages for many years.

From one point of view, one may say that the design goal of the language which was eventually to become Ada was simply to win the tender from the US Department of Defense. However, as a language which was the culmination of years of work all around the world, it had its own destiny to fulfil, as summed up in the single goal of concern for

- man – programming as a human activity;
- machine – efficient use of the resources of today's computers;
- management – control and care of large projects.

It is the aim of this chapter to show to what extent Ada has achieved these goals.

Data abstraction in Ada

The data abstraction facilities of Ada can be divided into those that are used in-the-small, and those that cater for programming in-the-large. The inner programming effort, where structured programming is now firmly entrenched, is served by

- type definitions,
- constraints,
- attributes.

In-the-large, we have four main facilities:

- packages,
- generics,
- tasks,
- exceptions.

Because Ada is Pascal-based, these are all supported by the usual infrastructure of Pascal, including

- procedures,
- functions,
- parameters,
- control structures,
- arithmetic,
- relations,

and so on. These will not be discussed in detail, and it is hoped that the reader will be interested enough by the development of the other features to pursue the study of Ada with the Manual [Department of Defense, 1983] or one of the books that are now being marketed [Barnes, 1984; Young, 1983; Gehani, 1983; Habermann and Perry, 1983]. Another excellent reference is the book of sample programs by Hibbard *et al.* [1981]. The only Ada feature that is not covered in this chapter is tasking, which is discussed in Chapter 6 on Concurrency.

4.2 Data abstraction in-the-small

It is not the function of this book to criticize Ada, nor have we found much to be critical of, but its type system strains the patience of even the most ardent supporter. Ada's types are defined in-the-small, i.e. simply as a set of values, with the operations being implied. On the face of it, there is a nice distinction between new types, which are all different and whose values cannot be mixed, and subtypes, whose values are compatible with their base types. But once one starts reading Chapter 3 of the Ada Manual and comes across predefined types, implementation defined types, universal types, model numbers, safe numbers, components and subcomponents, not to mention all the syntactic metaterms needed to describe combinations of all these, clarity flies out the window. If there is a better way of describing the same (admittedly very powerful) concepts, then it has not yet been written down, because all the textbooks dutifully follow the manual. The reader is thus left with the uncomfortable feeling that he is missing something if he doesn't understand the whole system all at once.

Since this book is based on the premise that one can reduce complexity by abstraction, we shall abstract away from all these confusing terms and simply present the essence of Ada's type system as it would appear to a working programmer. There are nuances that will be omitted, particularly in the numerical field, but what is given here is strictly correct, and is based on the experience of writing ordinary programs in Ada. The objective is to show that Ada is an advance over older languages, and does improve on Pascal, in spite of its seeming complexity.

Ada's type system

The Ada programmer is *given* the following types:

- integer
- float
- boolean
- character
- string

and he may *construct* new types using one of four methods:

- enumeration,
- array,
- record,
- access.

In so doing, he can specify that certain parts of the type are *variable*. The next step is to *refine* an existing type (given or constructed) by means of a constraint of which there are four, i.e.

- range,
- accuracy,
- indexed,
- discriminant.

When refining a type, one can choose to make the result one of a

- subtype, or
- derived type.

Subtypes are convenient in that they inherit all the properties of the original type. Derived types have the advantage that they can provide protection against accidental or intentional misuse of objects.

We shall now follow through the given types, the constructions, variations and refinements, using the data abstraction premise that a type is a set of values and the operations defined on them.

Given types

There are no surprises in the given types. Each has the usual

- range of values,
- notation for literals,
- operators,

that one expects from a high level language these days. Integers, for example, have the following operators

- relational : = /= < > <= >=
- arithmetic : abs − + * / ** mod rem

Unlike other languages, there are no other predefined functions, since the effect of these is achieved through the provision of all the properties of the type. Ada calls these properties *attributes*, and for integer, character and boolean types there are eleven available to the programmer. Some look like functions and take a parameter. The full list is given in Table 4.1. These attributes are very useful in writing general expressions. For example, to print out all the characters available, together with their equivalent numbers, we can say

```
FOR ch in character'first .. character'last LOOP
  put(ch); put(character'pos(ch));
END LOOP;
```

without knowing the numeric values in advance. Notice the syntax for using attributes entails writing the type name. Thus one must say integer'succ(i), not just succ(i).

Floating point numbers have attributes concerned with the accuracy

Table 4.1 Ada attributes

Attribute	*Parameter*	*Result*
base	—	a type
first	—	a value
last	—	a value
size	—	an integer
width	—	an integer
pos	a value	an integer
val	an integer	a value
succ	a value	a value
pred	a value	a value
image	a value	a string
value	a string	a value

necessary for fine numerical work. There is, incidentally, also a provision in Ada for fixed point numbers, but there is no given fixed point type: to use this facility, constraints must be specified, as discussed later.

There are no built-in input and output statements in Ada. For the given types, one must call in the text_io package which is done by saying

```
WITH text_io; USE text_io;
```

at the start of a program. The net effect of this is to make procedures such as get and put available for *characters and strings only*. For the other types, we must specialize the general features provided by text_io as follows:

```
PACKAGE int_io is NEW integer_io(integer); USE int_io;
PACKAGE flo_io is NEW float_io(float); USE flo_io;
PACKAGE boo_io is NEW enumeration_io(boolean); USE boo_io;
```

The pros and cons of this approach have been aired in Chapter 2, but further implications will become obvious when we look at subtypes versus derived types.

Constructing types

Enumerations, arrays, records and pointers are the classic ways of constructing the data structures used in modern programming practice. To form the new type, one gives the values it may have and, in the case of arrays and records, a definition of its structure. Examples are:

```
TYPE days      is (Sun, Mon, Tues, Wed, Thurs, Fri, Sat);
TYPE vowels    is ('A','E','I','O','U');
```

```
TYPE schedules  is array (days) of boolean;
TYPE vectors    is array (1..100) of integer;
TYPE cars       is RECORD
                     year : character;
                     number : integer;
                   END RECORD;
TYPE nodes;
TYPE tonodes    is access nodes;
TYPE nodes      is RECORD
                     left, right : tonodes;
                     data : character;
                   END RECORD;
```

Let us now consider the other properties, i.e.

- notation for literals,
- operators,
- attributes.

Unlike the older languages, Ada does provide for structured literals, known as aggregates, so that array and record variables can be assigned actual values, e.g.

```
v : vectors;
mycar : cars;
BEGIN
  v := (1..100 => 0);
  mycar := ('A', 304);
```

(There is more on aggregates in Chapter 2.)

As is to be expected, arrays and records have the equality and assignment operators defined, but Ada also permits other relations and catenation in certain cases. A very important aspect of arrays is that they can be *sliced* by specifying a range of elements.

One of the most powerful aids to data abstraction is the notion that types have properties – or attributes – that are available for examination, and this is particularly significant with arrays. For example, in FORTRAN, one would often write a subroutine to manipulate an array and pass both the array and its upper bounds as parameters, as in

```
FORTRAN: SUBROUTINE INVERT (A,N,M)
         DIMENSION A(N,M)
         DO 10 I = 1,N
         DO 20 J = 1,M
         ...
```

Even in Pascal, the array bounds are quite unconnected to the array itself and one is forced into defining myriad constants to give names to the limits.

```
Pascal: CONST n = ...;
              m = ...;
        VAR   a : array [1..n,1..m] of real;
              i : 1..n;
              j : 1..m;
        BEGIN
          FOR i := 1 to n do
            FOR j := 1 to m do
            ...
        END;
```

In Ada, the array's properties are given by four attributes, i.e.

first – lower bound
last – upper bound
length – number of elements
range – the subtype first..last

and each can be subscripted for a particular dimension. These attributes, however, apply to each array object, *not* each type. Thus we can examine v'first, but not vectors'first. Now suppose we define a matrix type and variable as

```
TYPE matrix is array (1..100,1..4) of integer;
m : matrix;
```

We don't have to define names for 100 and 4 because from now on we can refer to them as

```
m'last(1)   and   m'last(2)
```

where the subscripts indicate the dimension. As in Pascal, the size of the matrix is fixed at one place and if we wish to change it, we make the change there. No further changes need be made as the attributes will reflect the new values automatically. The range attribute is used for indices over the array and when these indices are part of a loop, they do not have to be separately declared. The little example in Pascal above becomes in Ada

```
DECLARE
  a : array (1..n, 1..m) of float;
  BEGIN
    FOR i in a'range(1) loop
      FOR j in a'range(2) loop
      ...
      end loop;
    end loop;
  END;
```

Variable types

One of the important features of Ada's array and record types is that they can vary in certain ways. In this, Ada has learnt from the deficiencies of Pascal and has provided flexibility, while maintaining strict security. There have been many calls for 'dynamic arrays' in Pascal, but with a good deal of confusion as to what exactly is required. In fact, there are two instances where variability is needed, and Ada provides for them by means of *dynamic* arrays and *unconstrained* arrays.

In Ada, declarations are considered to be executable. This is a major advance over Pascal and FORTRAN, and returns us to the Algol 60 era. In this way, an array can be declared with bounds which are variables, or even expressions. Then, provided the variables have values at the time that the declaration is executed, the array will assume the appropriate form. To ensure that the bounds are defined, they are declared in an outer level to the array. For example, suppose we have a simple test program that must read and write out two arrays of integers. The arrays may be of any size, and in Pascal one would be forced into specifying their upper bounds. In Ada, the program would be as in Figure 4.1. The variables a and b are examples of *dynamic arrays*. Notice that their types are anonymous. This is often the case with such arrays, and it is the only place where Ada permits anonymous or unnamed types.

The second instance when variability is needed is in defining a procedure that will work for arrays of different size. What we need here is an array type where the bounds are unspecified. In Ada, this is done by the phrase type RANGE <> – read 'type range box', and produces an *unconstrained array type*. Any variable with subscripts of a compatible type can then map onto type. For example, we can define read and write procedures which will cope with both of the arrays in the program of Figure 4.1, giving Figure 4.2.

```
WITH text_io;  USE text_io;

PROCEDURE array1 is
  PACKAGE int_io is new integer_io(integer); USE int_io;
  n, m : integer;
  BEGIN
    put_line(" How many elements in a and b?");
    get(n); get(m); skip_line;
    put(" n is "); put(n); put(" and m is "); put(m); new_line;
    DECLARE
      a : array (1..n) of integer;
      b : array (1..m) of integer;
    BEGIN
      for i in a'range loop get(a(i)); end loop; skip_line;
      for i in a'range loop put(a(i)); end loop; new_line;
      for i in b'range loop get(b(i)); end loop; skip_line;
      for i in b'range loop put(b(i)); end loop; new_line;
    END;
  END array1;
```

Figure 4.1 Example of dynamic arrays

```
WITH text_io; USE text_io;

PROCEDURE array2 is
  PACKAGE int_io is new integer_io(integer);  USE int_io;
  TYPE tables IS ARRAY (integer range <>) of integer;

  n, m : integer;

  PROCEDURE read (table : out tables) is
    BEGIN
      FOR i in table'range loop get(table(i)); end loop;
      skip_line;
    END read;

  PROCEDURE write (table : in tables) is
    BEGIN
      FOR i in table'range loop put(table(i)); end loop;
      new_line;
    END write;

  BEGIN
    put_line(" How many elements in a and b? ");
    get(n); get(m); skip_line;
    put(" n is "); put(n);  put(" m is "); put(m); new_line;
    DECLARE
      a : tables(1..n);
      b : tables(1..m);
    BEGIN
      read(a);
      write(a);
      read(b);
      write(b);
    END;
  END array2;
```

Figure 4.2 Example of unconstrained array types

To summarize, therefore, dynamic arrays enable one to have array objects of sizes specified at run-time; unconstrained arrays enable one to have array types that will accept array objects of any size.

The classic example of an unconstrained array type is the given type string which is defined for any integer subscripts from 1 upwards. Typically, one would define string variables as

```
s : string(1..80);
name : string (1..20);
```

Record objects can also vary in two ways by

- selecting one of a choice of field lists given in the type,
- providing a value for a dynamic array bound.

In the first case, the type gives the full choice of alternatives, together with a field which is the tag. When a record variable is declared, it must specify its choice by giving a value for the tag. This value may be a variable itself, but once declared it cannot be changed. The second case works just like dynamic arrays, but the bound is itself a field of the record. Here, a default initial value can be given for the bounds. Examples are given in Figure 4.3.

```
WITH text_io;  USE text_io;

PROCEDURE array3 is
  SUBTYPE natural is integer range
                      0..integer'last;              -- range constraint
  SUBTYPE real    is float digits 6;                -- digits constraint
  TYPE kinds      is (plain, decimal);              -- enumerated type
  TYPE itables    is array (integer range <>)
                      of natural;                   -- unconstrained
  TYPE rtables    is array (integer range <>)       --   array types
                      of real;
  TYPE tablepack
      (length : integer := 100;                     -- bound discriminant
       kind   : kinds := plain) is                  -- variant discriminant
      RECORD
        CASE kind is                                -- variant choice
          WHEN plain =>
                itable : itables (1..length);       -- indexed constraint
          WHEN decimal =>
                rtable : rtables (1..length);       -- indexed constraint
        END CASE;
      END RECORD;

  PACKAGE real_io is new float_io(real);            -- i/o instantiations
  PACKAGE int_io  is new integer_io(integer);       --   for real, integer
  USE real_io, int_io;                              --   and their subtypes

  n, m : integer;

  BEGIN
    put_line(" How many elements in a and b?");
    get(n); get(m);  skip_line;
    put(" n has "); put(n); put(" and m has "); put(m); new_line;
    DECLARE
      a : tablepack (n, plain);                   -- creating dynamic
      b : tablepack (m, decimal);                 --   arrays with variants
    BEGIN
      for i in a.itable'range loop get(a.itable(i)); end loop; skip_line;
      for i in a.itable'range loop put(a.itable(i),6); end loop;new_line;
      for i in b.rtable'range loop get(b.rtable(i)); end loop; skip_line;
      for i in b.rtable'range loop put(b.rtable(i),6); end loop;new_line;
    END;
  END array3;
```

Figure 4.3 Example of constraints

Refined types

Just as one may wish parts of a type to vary, so one may wish to give a name to a chosen variation. In so doing, one must decide whether the new type is a subtype or a derived type. The choice is really very simple. Subtypes are in all senses more convenient because the new type inherits all the operations that were defined for the original. In particular, it will inherit any input/output packages that were instantiated. On the other hand, we know that data abstraction enables conceptually different types to have the same representation, but one would not wish objects of such types to be intermingled. In this case, one can derive a new type, the effect of which is to exclude any operations that were not specifically defined along with the original. The possible refinements are:

1. *Range constraint.* Integer, character, enumerated, fixed and floating types can be restricted to a certain range.
2. *Accuracy constraint.* Floating numbers can have the number of decimal digits of accuracy given and fixed types can have the delta or increment between values specified.
3. *Indexed constraint.* A new type can be refined from an unconstrained array type by giving suitable bounds.
4. *Discriminant constraint.* A new type can be refined from a variable record type by specifying values for any of the tag or array bound fields. (However, either all or none of the values must be given.)

As an example, suppose we wish to keep the length of our arrays with the array, and also to have arrays of positive integers or of real numbers with six digits of accuracy. A program to define such a structure with all the associated types and subtypes, suitably annotated, and to read and write a couple of arrays as before would be as in Figure 4.3.

Using types, subtypes and attributes

To sum up the power of Ada's type system, we can say that it

- forces connections between names referring to objects of the same type and their common properties;
- prevents interaction between objects that have been consciously declared as having completely different types, even though some of the properties may be similar;
- keeps the number of names required to achieve this to a minimum.

These points are illustrated in the following example.

Set up a type called tables which has elements of any type, item, and bounds of any discrete type (integer or enumerated). Write two procedures

- read: reads in a variable number of items until either the table is full or some trailer value is spotted, in which case the table is padded with the trailer.
- write: writes out the full table.

To solve the problem, we assume a global variable, trailer, and a definition for tables as follows:

```
TYPE tables is array (bounds) of item;
```

Then the two routines are as given in Figure 4.4. This example illustrates two very common types of loops. In read we have the loop with two terminating conditions, and one of them requires a follow-up loop. Write has a simple counting loop over an entire range. The solution assumes nothing about the type, bounds, other than that it is a valid type for

```
PROCEDURE  read (table :out tables) is
  TYPE states is (reading,ended ,filled);
  i            : bounds := table'first;
  state        : states :=reading;

  BEGIN
    LOOP
      get(table(i));
      if    i = table'last   then state:=filled;
      elsif table(i)=trailer then state:=ended; end if;
      if    state/=filled    then i:=bounds'succ(i); end if;
      EXIT when state/=reading;
    END LOOP;

    WHILE state/=filled loop
      table(i):=trailer;
      if i=table'last then state:=filled;
                      else i:=bounds'succ(i);
      end if;
    END LOOP;
  END read;

PROCEDURE write (table:tables) is
  BEGIN
    for i in bounds loop
      put(' '); put(table(i));
    end loop;
  END write;
```

Figure 4.4 Reading and writing arrays

an array subscript, and that succ is defined for it. This level of abstraction is achieved largely by accepting that array bounds should be a data type, and by the extension of this idea to type attributes. However, the logic of the loop and the use of a state variable also contribute to the success of the read procedure.

These procedures therefore represent quite a powerful piece of programming from the maintainability and protection viewpoints; they are also very versatile, in that we could use them for quite different arrays, as in

```
-- An array of reals
   TYPE      item   is digits 6;
   SUBTYPE bounds is integer range 1..100;

   trailer : constant item := 0.0;
   marks : tables;

     read(marks);  -- will read up to 100 marks and pad any
                   -- left over slots with 0.
```

or in

```
-- An array of strings indexed by an enumerated type
   TYPE      bounds is (Britain, France, Spain, Italy);
   SUBTYPE item      is string(1..8);

   trailer : constant item := "        ";
   towns : tables;

     read(towns);  -- will read up to 20 towns and pad any
                   -- left over slots with blanks.
```

4.3 Data abstraction in-the-large

So far we have been concerned with individual data types and how they are manipulated in an easy and secure way, and we end up with features very much at the level of structured programming. Ada's brief extends much further into the realm of large programming projects, with perhaps many programmers involved on different interconnecting tasks. The key to secure management of such a project lies in being able to divide up the tasks logically, and then use the language to implement them. The facility provided by Ada for this purpose is the *package*.

The structure of an Ada package is illustrated in Figure 4.5. The package starts off with a specification of its data and operations. This is followed by an optional section indicating those parts of the data that will be known to the outside world by name, but cannot be examined in detail. The package body then repeats the specifications, filling out each with the required implementation.

Ada's packages serve data abstraction at three levels.

1. Named collections of declarations. In other languages, this facility is often provided by file 'includes' and a preprocessor.
2. Groups of logically related subprograms sharing internal declarations. This is the one facility which the traditional block-structured languages could not provide. In Ada, the package idea breaks away from strict nesting.
3. Encapsulated data types with hidden implementations of operations. This is data abstraction in its full sense, providing economy of effort, ease of maintenance and as much protection as is required.

The examples that follow illustrate each of these levels. But first we

```
PACKAGE name is
  -- types, variables, procedures and
  --   functions for the package.
PRIVATE
  -- details of those types which need to be hidden.
END name;
```

```
PACKAGE BODY name is
  -- declarations of local types, variables, etc.;
  -- implementations of procedures and functions
  --    mentioned in the specification.
END name;
```

Figure 4.5 The structure of a package

must detail the ways in which packages are actually used. There are three ways:

1. Access to all names in the package by

```
USE table_manager;
IF table_full then ...
```

2. Access to only selected names by using dot notation

```
IF table_manager.table_full then ...
```

3. Shorthand for selected names by using renames

```
full : boolean renames table_manager.table_full;
IF full then ...
```

In all these cases, the statement

```
WITH table_manager;
```

is also necessary to give access to the unit as stored in an Ada library.

Examples of groups and collections

1. Named collections of declarations.

```
WITH codehandler;
PACKAGE employeedata is
  TYPE dates is ....;
  TYPE money is delta 0.01 range 0..100_000.0;
  TYPE addresses is array (1..4) of string (1..20);
  TYPE employees is record
        key             : codehandler.employeecode;
        name            : string(1..25);
        address         : addresses;
        birth, marriage: dates;
        salary          : money;
  END RECORD;
```

2. Group of related subprograms.

```
PACKAGE printunit is
  PROCEDURE newpage;
  PROCEDURE newline;
  PROCEDURE print (ch : in character);
  PROCEDURE tab (n : natural);
  PROCEDURE startprinting;
  PROCEDURE stopprinting;
END printunit;
PACKAGE BODY printunit is
  TYPE linerange is new integer range 1..132;
  TYPE pagerange is new integer range 1..10000;
  TYPE lines is array (linerange) of character;
  TYPE pages is array (pagerange) of lines;
  TYPE columns is new integer range 1..4;
```

```
      tray            : array(columns) of pages;
      currentcolumn   : columns;
      currentline     : pagerange;
      currentchar     : linerange;
    PROCEDURE newline is
      BEGIN
        currentline := currentline + 1;
        if currentline = pagerange'last then newpage; end if;
      END newline;
    -- etc.
  END printunit;
```

Encapsulated data types

So far, packages have given us the ability to have

- *visible* data in the specification, and
- *invisible* data in the body.

Thus, in the second example above, only the procedures were relevant to a user; the line positions and the actual storing of the characters to be printed were entirely private and protected. The third kind of abstraction mixes the visibility so that we have PRIVATE data which has

- *visible* names in the specification, and
- *invisible* implementations in the body.

There are several reasons for making this separation. The best one is that it gives the ability to change one's mind about an implementation without affecting all the other programs that might be using the package.

Suppose a firm sets up codes for all its employees. It may decide after a few years that the code has to be expanded because there are now too many employees. A package can be set up which defines the concept of an employee code, together with the ability to make and compare them, but keeps the actual form of the code hidden.

```
PACKAGE codehandler is
  TYPE employeecode is private;
  PROCEDURE makecode (n : out employeecode);
  FUNCTION "<"      (n,m : in employeecode) return boolean;
```

An application programmer who is writing the program to set up new employees would be able to declare an employeecode, call the makecode routine to get a value for it, and store it away. Another programmer who is writing a merge, say, would need to compare codes, and could do this using <. He would, of course, get the full details of the whole employee record from another package of the first kind above in which the full layout is defined. A start to such a merge might be

```
WITH employeedata, codehandler, text_io;
USE employeedata, codehandler, text_io;
PROCEDURE merge is
  -- declarations of files viz. master, update : filetype;
  e1, e2 : employees;
  BEGIN
    -- open files;
    LOOP
      get(master, e1);
      get(update, e2);
      if e1.key < e2.key then ...
      ...
      end if;
    END LOOP;
    -- close files
  END merge;
```

The actual form of the code is declared later in the package, together with the implementations of the two routines.

```
PRIVATE
  TYPE employeecode is
          range 000_000 .. 999_999;
END codehandler;
PACKAGE BODY codehandler is
  currentcode : employeecode;
  PROCEDURE makecode (n : out employeecode) is
    BEGIN
      n := currentcode;
      currentcode := currentcode + 1;
    END makecode;
  FUNCTION "<" (n,m : in employeecode) RETURN boolean is
    BEGIN
      return n < m;
    END "<";
  PROCEDURE get (f : filetype; e : out employees) is
    -- as required
  END codehandler;
```

The fact that the code is actually a number is quite hidden from the applications programmers. At a later date it could be changed into an alphanumeric code, in which case the makenumber and < routines will become more complex.

The second reason for encapsulating data types in packages is security. Once a type is private, the only valid operations are

- declare an object, e.g. c1, c2 : employeecode;
- assignment, e.g. mycode := c1;
- compare for equality, e.g. if c1=c2 then ...

- use as parameters, e.g. PROCEDURE fire (h : employeecode)
- packaged operations, e.g. makecode and <

This list excludes the ability to make constants of the type (which would be impossible because the actual form is hidden), access components (if applicable) or do any other operations not in the package (such as writing out the code). Even if a programmer knew or suspected that the code was simply a number, and attempted to say

```
mycode := 546789;
```

or

```
put (mycode); -- i.e. print it.
```

the compiler would prevent him. Since it may be possible by devious use of assignment, procedures and equality to fabricate, inspect and change codes, Ada provides a further level of protection called LIMITED PRIVATE which removes all the above rights. Limited private objects can only be declared and used with the operations provided.

Generalizing packages

One of the obvious powers of packages is that they can become like standard utilities which can be used over and over again by many people. For this to be really effective, something must be done about allowing the package to perform its action on data of various kinds. For example, we might set up a very efficient merge sort package, but want the details of the records being sorted to remain unspecified in the package itself. Then when a programmer wishes to use the package, he says at that stage what the data looks like. This facility is in fact generalizing the package idea and is provided in Ada through generic packages.

Figure 4.6 shows the structure of a generic package. In the first place, the package is written in a general way and the parts that can vary are specified. When the package is to be used, these parts are filled in and the package is then said to be *instantiated*. The routines of the package are then executed as required.

A very good example of a package that would benefit from generalization is the pair of routines defined in Figure 4.4. The examples at the end of Section 4.2 showed different definitions for item and bounds, implying in fact that the procedures would have to be completely written out in each case. Figure 4.7 shows how a generic package would do the trick. It includes two completely different instantiations, for strings and for real vectors as well as a main procedure to call the subprograms. (The reason for including package reals is given under the discussion on overloading, below.)

We notice in passing that the iterator as defined accepts only

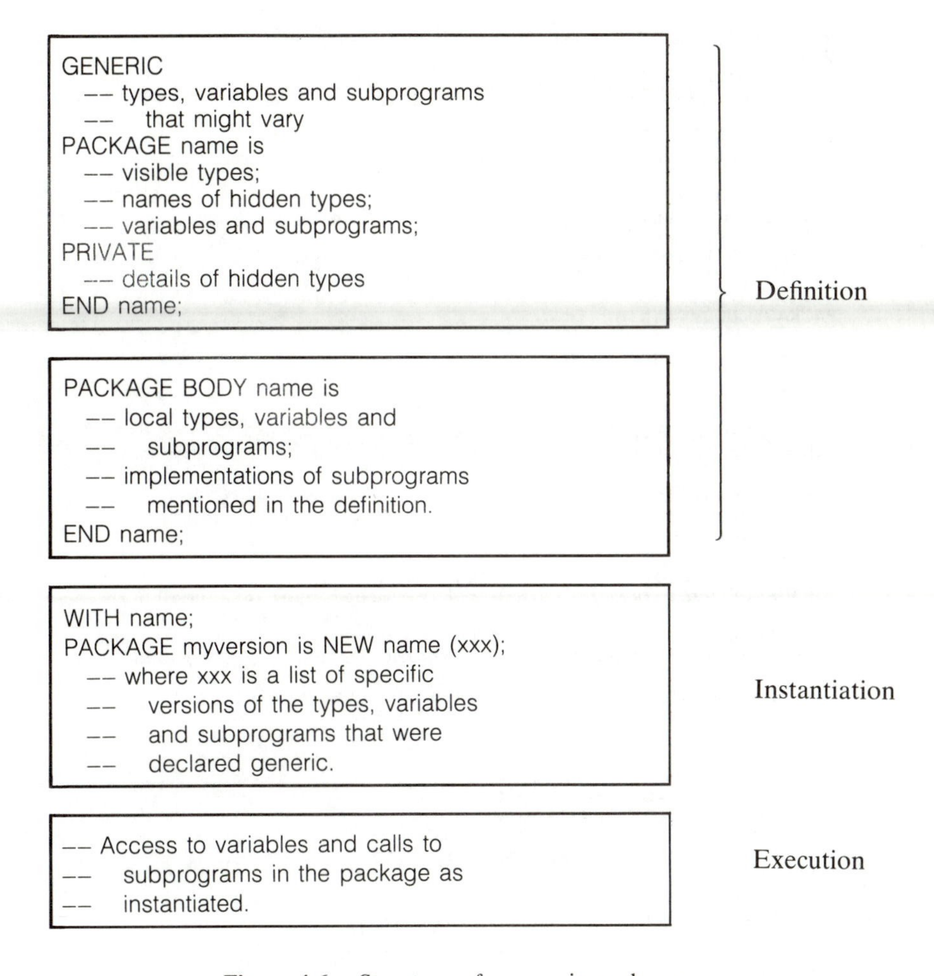

Figure 4.6 Structure of a generic package

constrained arrays; as explained in the *Ada Manual* (Section 12.3.4) [Department of Defense, 1983], a package accepting unconstrained arrays would have to have a definition for tables with bounds specified as "range <>", which would confine the subscripts to integers or enumerateds but not both. There are various ways in which the generic part can indicate what actual parameters would be suitable (see Table 4.2). Note that the use of the word PRIVATE in the generic part is strictly in the 'yet to be specified' sense rather than in 'needs to be hidden' sense.

Overloading

In these examples, we have used a facility without explaining it. This is the ability to have the same name stand for different operations. In the example of Figure 4.7 read was used to read towns and read marks. In fact the actual

```
WITH text_io;  USE text_io; --to use 'get' and 'put'
GENERIC
   TYPE item     is private;
   TYPE bounds   is (<>);
        trailer : item;
   WITH PROCEDURE get(i : out item) is <>;
   WITH PROCEDURE put(i : in item)  is <>;

PACKAGE tabler is
   TYPE       tables is array(bounds) of item;
   PROCEDURE read(table:out tables);
   PROCEDURE write(table:in tables);
END tabler;

PACKAGE BODY tabler is

    -- as in Figure 4.4

END tabler;

WITH text_io, tabler, reals; USE text_io, reals;
PROCEDURE readtables is

   -- Instantiation of tabler for an array of reals.
   --    Uses the reals package which has single parameter
   --    get and put procedures.

   SUBTYPE vectorrange is integer range 1..10;
   PACKAGE vectormaker is NEW tabler (real,vectorrange,0.0);

   -- Instantiation of tabler for an array of strings indexed
   --    by an enumerated type.  String_io already included in text_io.

   TYPE    countries   is (Britain, France, Spain, Italy);
   SUBTYPE names       is string(1..8);
   PACKAGE stringmaker is NEW tabler (names,countries,"        ",
                                      get, put_line);

    towns : stringmaker.tables;
    marks : vectormaker.tables;

    USE stringmaker, vectormaker;
  BEGIN
    read(towns);
    write(towns);
    read(marks);
    write(marks);
  END readtables;


DATA                                        RESULTS
====                                        =======

London  Paris   Madrid  Rome                London
5.6                                         Paris
7.8                                         Madrid
9.4                                         Rome
0.0                                              5.599E+00
                                                 7.799E+00
                                                 9.399E+00
                                                 0.000E+00
                                                 0.000E+00
                                                 0.000E+00
                                                 0.000E+00
                                                 0.000E+00
                                                 0.000E+00
                                                 0.000E+00
```

Figure 4.7 Example of a generic package and its use

Table 4.2 Possibilities for generic types

Formal	*Actual*
TYPE t is limited private;	any, but no assignment implied
TYPE t is private;	any except limited private
TYPE t (...) is private;	any with a matching discriminant
TYPE t is (<>)	discrete
TYPE t is range <>;	integer
TYPE t is digits <>;	floating
TYPE t is delta <>;	fixed
TYPE t is array ...	array
TYPE t is access A;	access

routines called are quite different, each belonging to one of the instantiations of the tabler package. Because towns and marks are of different types, Ada can work out which version of read is required. This is called overloading a name. Notice that overloading is possible only if there is no ambiguity. At the point where the variables marks and towns are declared it is necessary to be explicit about which tables type is being referred to. If the references to tables had not been prefixed by the appropriate package name, the compiler would have reported an error.

Overloading of subprograms requires that the number of parameters in the actual subprograms matches that in the formal. Unfortunately, this raises a side problem with the input and output in the read and write procedures above. The problem seems trivial, but has to be overcome at some length. In the text_io package supplied for Ada, get and put for reals are defined with two or three parameters, although all but one can be defaulted. Therefore, a version does not exist that is compatible with that for strings and characters. Consequently, instead of relying on overloading for get and put, we have to add these subprograms to the generic part and instantiate them accordingly.

The string instantiation passes get and put_line across, with Ada working out that the string versions of these from text_io are the ones being referred to. For the instantiation involving reals, we first define a little package that has the required single parameter versions of get and put and simply calls the built-in versions appropriately, i.e.

```
WITH text_io; USE text_io;
PACKAGE reals is
  TYPE real is digits 6;
  PROCEDURE get (r : out real);
  PROCEDURE put (r : in real);
END reals;
PACKAGE BODY reals is
  PACKAGE real_io is new float_io(real);
```

```
    PROCEDURE get (r : out real) is
      BEGIN
        real_io.get(r);
      END get;
    PROCEDURE put (r : in real) is
      BEGIN
        real_io.put(r,6,3); new_line;
      END put;
  END reals;
```

In the instantiation we do not have to mention get and put as the box <> in the generic part is effectively a default and will match with any compatible and visible subprogram of the same name.

Ada's exception system

The presence of possible exception conditions must be declared by means of a declaration in the appropriate subprogram, such as

```
parity_error : EXCEPTION;
```

There are five predefined exceptions in Ada, viz.

- constraint_error – if a constraint on a value is violated,
- numeric_error – if a numeric operation overflows or underflows,
- program_error – if a called program unit has not yet been elaborated,
- storage_error – if an attempt is made to exceed the available storage,
- tasking_error – if an error occurs in inter-task communication.

Exceptions, both user-defined and pre-defined, may be raised by interrupts from the run-time systems or through device drivers or other low level routines, or they may be raised explicitly in the program by using a RAISE statement. The RAISE statement may specify the name of the exception to be raised, or it can be used on its own, in which case it causes the last raised exception to be re-raised.

Once an exception has been raised, the Ada system will look for a handler. It starts looking in the current block and proceeds outwards until, in the absence of any handler, the program will be terminated. Handlers consist of statements at the end of a block introduced by the word EXCEPTION followed by WHEN exception_name => for each one. Lists of names can be given, and the catch-all OTHERS is also permitted. For example, consider the following Ada block (from Booch [1983]):

```
DECLARE
  low_fluid_level : EXCEPTION;
BEGIN
  -- statements which may cause a numeric error, and
  -- which include a
  RAISE low_fluid_level;
```

```
  -- somewhere.
EXCEPTION
  WHEN low_fluid_level =>
    open_valve;
    sound_alarm;
  WHEN numeric_error =>
    raise;
  WHEN others =>
    log_unknown_error;
END;
```

If the statements calculate that the fluid level is low, or if this is indicated by some external device, then control passes to the exception handler labelled low_fluid_level and the statements there are executed. If the calculations result instead in a numeric_error, control is transferred to the second handler, which simply propagates the exception to the next level up. If any other exception is raised, it is handled by logging the fact, and then the block is exited as before. In other words, the handler effectively clears the exception and, unless there is a re-raise, no further action at a higher level is required.

The important points about Ada's exception handlers are that

- they operate within the same environment as that in which the exception occurred; and
- they effectively replace the statements that would otherwise have been executed.

These are ideal conditions for recovery operations.

Typically, the response to an exception falls into one of four categories:

- abandon any further action,
- try again,
- repair the error and try again,
- try an alternative approach.

These are illustrated by a series of examples from Booch [1983]. In all but the first, loops or recursion need to be brought into play – a fact that is often not appreciated by newcomers to exception handling. The classic example of the 'try again' case is the handling of invalid data, as in

```
TYPE response is (up, down, left, right);
user_request : response;
LOOP
  BEGIN
    put ('>');
    get(user_request);   -- could cause a data_error;
    exit;                -- the loop if all alright
  EXCEPTION
    WHEN data_error =>
      put_line("Invalid response. Enter one of UP, DOWN, LEFT, RIGHT");
  END;
END LOOP;
```

The repair option works well with recursion, as shown in this example:

```
PROCEDURE move_rudder (amount : in out integer) is
  rudder_stressed : exception;
  BEGIN
    -- statements to send commands to the rudder
    -- which may interrupt with the exception
  EXCEPTION
    WHEN rudder_stressed =>
      amount := amount / 2;
      if amount /= 0
        then move_rudder(amount);
        else raise;
      end if;
  END move_rudder;
```

Here the parameter to the procedure is adjusted in the handler, and if still appropriate, the procedure is simply reactivated. Otherwise, the exception is propagated to the calling environment. The last option, that of trying an alternative strategy, is shown in this example using tasking:

```
send_message : array (1..10) of message_task;
FOR i in 1..10
LOOP
  BEGIN
    send_message (i) (critical_message);
    exit;
  EXCEPTION
    WHEN tasking_error =>
      if i < 10
        then null;
        else send_alert_to_operator;
             raise;
      end if;
  END;
END LOOP;
```

Here there are ten identical tasks which are tried in turn, and as soon as one accepts the message the loop is exited. If the task does not accept the message, the exception is raised but effectively nothing happens until we have tried the last task. In that case, an alert is signalled and the exception is propagated up.

Exception handling is a difficult area of programming and there is not much in the literature on practice and experience, but see Bron and Dijkstra [1986]. There is still a great deal of discussion on the language forms and semantics associated with exceptions, and this is covered in Section 7.5.

Exercises

1. Write an essay on the data abstraction facilities provided by Ada. Pay particular attention to the different uses of data abstraction, the levels of visibility provided, the implications for compiler writers and the provisions made for generic program units.
2. 'User-defined types are second-class citizens in Ada.' Discuss this statement and show how rights not naturally available to user types can be acquired by means of overloading and generics.
3. Gries and Gehani [1977] noted two important properties of programming languages:
   - the domain of an array should be a data type,
   - procedures should work for parameterized types.

   Discuss the features that Ada provides to realize these goals, with particular reference to improvements on earlier languages.

References

Ambler, A.L., Good, D.I., Browne, J.C., Burger, W.F., Cohen, R.M., Hoch, C.G. and Wells, R.E., 1977. 'GYPSY: A language for the specification and implementation of verifiable programs', *SIGPLAN*, **12(3)**, 1–10.

Barnes, J.G.P., 1980. 'An overview of Ada', *SPE*, **10(11)**, 851–887.

Barnes, J.G.P., 1984. *Programming in Ada*, 2nd edn., London, Addison-Wesley.

Booch, G., 1983. *Software Engineering with Ada*, Menlo Park. CA, Benjamin/Cummings.

Bron, C. and Dijkstra, E.J., 1986. 'On the use of exception handling in Modular Pascal', Proceedings of the IFIP WG2.4 Symposium on *Systems Implementation Languages – Experience and Assessment*, Canterbury, UK, September 1985, Amsterdam, North-Holland, in press.

Clark, B.L. and Horning, J.J., 1971. 'The system language for programming SUE', *SIGPLAN*, **6(9)**, 79–88.

Department of Defense, 1983. *Military Standard for the Ada Programming Language*, MIL-STD-1815A.

Gehani, N., 1983. *Ada, an Advanced Introduction*, New Jersey, Prentice-Hall.

Gries, D. and Gehani, N., 1977. 'Some ideas on data types in high-level languages', *CACM*, **20(6)**, 414–420.

Habermann, A.N. and Perry, D.E., 1983. *Ada for Experienced Programmers*, Reading, MA, Addison-Wesley.

Hibbard, P., Hisgen, A., Rosenberg, J., Shaw, M. and Sherman, M., 1981. *Studies in Ada Style*, New York, Springer-Verlag.

Ichbiah, J., Rissen, J.P., Heliard, J.C. and Cousot, P., 1974. *The Systems Implementation Language LIS*, CII-HB Report 4549 E/EN (Part II), CII-Honeywell-Bull, Louveciennes, France.

Ichbiah, J., Heliard, J.C., Roubine, O., Barnes, J.G.P., Krieg-Bruckner, B. and Wichmann, B.A., 1979. 'Rationale for the programming language Ada', *SIGPLAN*, **14(6B)**.

Lampson, B.W., Horning, J.J., London, R.L., Mitchell, J.G. and Popek, G.J., 1977. 'Report on the programming language EUCLID', *SIGPLAN*, **12(2)**, 1–79.

Liskov, B.H., Snyder, A. and Atkinson, R., 1977. 'Abstraction mechanisms in CLU', *CACM*, **20(8)**, 564–576.

Moffat, D.V., 1981. 'A model for Pascal-like typing', *SIGPLAN*, **16(7)**, 66–74.

Redwine, S.J., 1981. 'A paradigm for dealing with exceptions', *SIGPLAN*, **16(5)**, 36–38.

Shaw, M., Wulf, W.A. and London, R.L., 1976. 'Introduction to construction and verification of Alphard programs', *IEEE-SE*, **2(4)**, 253–265 (also in *Alphard: Form and Content*, edited by Mary Shaw, New York, Springer-Verlag, 1981).

SIGPLAN, 1976. Conference on Data: Abstraction, Definition and Structure, *SIGPLAN*, **11**, special issue.

SIGPLAN, 1977. Conference on Language Design for Reliable Software, *SIGPLAN*, **12(3)** (also as *SIGOPS*, **11(2)** and *SIGSOFT* **2(2)**).

Wirth, N., 1971. 'The programming language Pascal', *Acta Informatica*, **1**, 35–63.

Wirth, N., 1976. 'Programming languages – what to demand and how to assess them', *Proceedings of the Symposium on Software Engineering*, BCS, Belfast, April 1976.

Wirth, N., 1977. 'The Modula Papers', *SPE*, **7(1)**, 3–84.

Young, S.J., 1983. *An Introduction to Ada*, Chichester, Ellis Horwood.

Chapter 5 Iterators and Generators

In earlier chapters we concentrated on data abstraction and the incorporation of data types into the language at the procedural level. The next step is to consider the place of new data types in the 'inner language'; that is, its control structure. The archetypal control structure is the loop, requiring as it does variables as well as values of the data type to be given. In this chapter we look at iterators which specify the basic elements of loop control and investigate generators which enable interaction with new data types.

5.1 Iterators

An iterator in its basic form is simply a loop construct. All imperative languages have them, but the variety of facilities is wide. When analysing the action of iterators, or loops, we usually start by classifying them according to the accepted syntactic forms. So we speak of FOR or DO loops, and know that they involve counting, and of WHILE or REPEAT loops that imply the testing of conditions. In prestructured programming days, there would also be loops constructed with IFs and GOTOs which then might fall into either category. The essence of a loop is, however, independent of actual constructs or classifications, and was first examined in a comprehensive paper by Pratt [1978].

Central to the understanding of a loop is the identification of the *control flow* and the *control computation*. When identifying control flow, we look for where the *body* of the loop starts and ends and whether there are other *entries* and *exits* to it. For control computation, we look for the *variables* used in controlling the loop, and endeavour to find the places where they are *initialized*, *altered* and *checked* for termination. For example, consider the loops in Figure 5.1.

Analysing these loops informally, we notice the following.

1. *A FOR loop*. The control flow is obvious and so is the control computation. The loop starts at the FOR and ends with the END. The variable used, its initialization and termination condition are clearly stated. The altering of the variable by one is not stated, but is successfully implied. FOR loops are generally the easiest to understand but their area of application is limited to deterministic cases.

1. Pascal:
```
{Read and sum 10 numbers}
sum := 0;
FOR i := 1 to 10 do begin
  read(n);
  sum := sum + n;
END;
```

2. Pascal:
```
{Find the last non-space in a string}
i := length(s);
WHILE (i > 1) and (s[i] <> space) do
  i := i - 1;
```

3. Ada:
```
{Read characters into a string until a space}
i := s'first;
LOOP
  get(ch);
  EXIT WHEN ch = space;
  s(i) := ch;
  EXIT WHEN i = s'last;
  i := i+1;
END LOOP;
```

4. BASIC:
```
200 REM GETS A YES OR NO REPLY
210 INPUT A$
220 IF A$ = "YES" GOTO 300
230 IF A$ = "NO" GOTO 400
240 PRINT "ANSWER YES OR NO"
250 GO TO 210
```

Figure 5.1 Examples of loops

2. *A* WHILE *loop*. Once again, the control flow is obvious, and so in this case is the control computation: it is clear that i is the loop variable, that it is initialized just before the loop begins, is altered once during the loop and is used in two checks for termination. However, here we have a very small loop and in larger ones it may well happen that the altering is divorced from the WHILE part of the loop. There may even be more than one statement that alters the loop variable. In the same vein, there is nothing to keep the initializing of i alongside the WHILE and it may occur anywhere. A great source of error in this kind of loop is a failure to include the initialization at all! In total, therefore, only the termination condition is obvious, giving quite a poor score for control computation here.
3. *An* EXIT WHEN *loop*. In this Ada loop there are two termination conditions which appear as EXIT WHEN statements within the loop body. The initialization and altering once again stand alone. Since one would have to scan the body to find such statements, control computation scores almost zero in such loops. Control flow is adequate, with LOOP-END LOOP marking the body and the EXIT WHENs indicating the exits.

4. *An IF GOTO loop*. When studying this loop, which exhibits typical BASIC programming, we find that the control flow is not obvious at all. There are two exit points and the start of the loop is not defined (in all likelihood the loop is entered at line 240 rather than line 210). The control computation is spread over three statements, none of which is specially identifiable as belonging to a loop.

From the above we can see that, without a special loop construct, the elements of loop control are completely dispersed: one has to scan the program and even draw a flowchart to discover the very existence of a loop. Fortunately, that is behind us now and constructs in modern languages have at least the following two properties in the control flow:

1. The *body* of the loop is contiguous and clearly visible, being delimited by keywords and, by convention, indented.
2. *Entry* to a loop is at the start of the body only.

However, the position, number and identity of the exits vary giving:

1. *Exit position*. The main exit of a loop is implied and coincides with the end of the body. If there are other explicit exits, they may occur anywhere in the body.
2. *Exit number*. Languages either specify no extra exits (rare) or place no restriction on the number.
3. *Exit identity*. Older languages permitted the use of the GOTO for additional exits from a loop. Although Knuth [1974], in his classic paper on structured programming with GOTO statements, advocates the use of GOTOs for this purpose, they are now generally discouraged. The fashion is to provide an EXIT WHEN statement which is readily identifiable as a loop exit and in some languages (Ada) may be further qualified by the name of the loop, e.g.

```
search: LOOP
    .
    .
    EXIT search WHEN ...
    .
END LOOP search;
```

Pratt [1978] discusses control flow in more detail, criticizing especially languages where loops have to be constructed using IFs and GOTOs. For such a loop, none of the elements of loop control is identifiable and even the existence of a loop is not obvious. It is strange therefore that the designers of FORTRAN 77 did not see the need for a second loop construct to enable conditional loops to have proper bodies.

One important aspect of control flow not specifically identified by Pratt is the loop's *follow-up*. Particularly when a loop has multiple exits, there are likely to be certain operations to perform in tidying up loose ends and bringing all the paths through the loop to a common point. Since termination conditions are involved as well, we shall discuss follow-ups fully in the following section on control computation.

The subject of control flow is not limited to loops and much has been written about the structured and unstructured nature of programs. Provided that one permits the program flow to be altered, then it has been shown [Bohm and Jacopini, 1966] that any unstructured program can be converted into a structured one comprising a finite number of basic elements, each with a single entry and a single exit. If therefore one values the property of a single exit from a loop, one can theoretically achieve it for any initially multi-exit solution.

5.2 Control computation

A loop starts in a certain state and is executed until another state is reached. The control computation consists of

- identifying
- initializing
- altering
- checking

the variables involved in this state. There is a tremendous variation in the support provided by control constructs for these elements. In general, the counting loops come out quite well: all four elements appear in the usual FOR-type statements, and these statements are present in almost every language. However, conditional loops are very poorly provided for. Few versions of the WHILE or REPEAT constructs provide any assistance in identifying loop variables or in initializing and altering them. Each element will now be considered in detail.

Identifying loop variables

In current counting loop constructs, there is only one loop variable and it is clearly identified at the start of the loop, as in

```
Pascal: FOR i := 1 to 100 do ...
```

The interesting points centre around the *scope* and *availability* of this loop variable. In older languages such as FORTRAN, the loop variable has a scope within the subprogram containing the loop and may be accessed and altered anywhere there. Pascal was more careful and said that the loop variable should not be altered within the loop. (It was the responsibility of implementors to devise a way of enforcing this rule.) Both Algol 68 and Ada decided that this was not enough and confined the scope of the variable to the loop itself by implicitly declaring it at the FOR clause.

This last restriction on scope is not helpful. It seems to have been introduced in order to enforce the ban on altering, but it leads to problems in multi-exit loops, where the follow-up to a loop may well need the value of the loop variable in order to be able to perform its work. This topic is discussed later, but as far as loop variable identification goes, the language CHILL seems to have a viable solution. CHILL states that the loop variable is implicitly defined at the start of the loop, but if a variable of the same name is declared in a surrounding scope, then, on an abnormal exit (i.e. a jump out of the loop), this variable will contain the value of the loop variable at that time. For a normal exit, the value of the outer variable would be undefined. This seems to give the best of both worlds – the loop variable itself is protected, but its value is available after the loop when appropriate.

Still on counting loops, the question should be asked as to why only one variable is permitted. If two data structures are being processed at the same time and both have determinable ranges (i.e. they are not linked lists) one should be able to give both ranges and appropriate indices at the start of the loop. For example, one would like to write

```
FOR i := 1 to 26 and for ch := 'a' to 'z' do
  count(i) := frequency[ch];
```

Instead, one has to treat one of the structures differently as follows:

```
Pascal: ch := 'a';
        FOR i := 1 to 26 do begin
          count[i] := frequency[ch];
          if ch <> 'z' then ch := succ(ch);
        END;
```

The restriction on multiple loop variables is probably due to a concern for the semantics of loop termination: with more than one counter, does the loop end when any or all are done? With a bit of thought it is clear that the answer must be any, because the data structure indexed by the shortest loop variable may not be defined over a longer range. The semantics would have to be very carefully defined, though, to ensure that all the variables were altered before any of the checks done, so that in the event of an exit from the loop, the variables will all correctly reflect the number of times that the loop was executed. CHILL is one language which has this feature.

In the same way, there are cases where no loop variable is necessary. For example, in printing *n* dashes, one would like to say, as in Algol 68,

```
Algol 68: from 1 to 10 do write(dash) od;
```

or better still

```
Algol 68: to 10 do write(dash) od;
```

Similarly, the FOR loop example in Figure 5.1 could be written as

```
Algol 68: sum := 0;
          to 10 do
            read(n);
            sum +:= n;
          od;
```

Unless a data structure is being iterated over, there is no need for a variable and all that is required is a simple count. Although simple to implement, few other languages provide this facility. (COBOL does.)

In summary, we make the following three points:

1. It is good to *forbid altering* of the loop variable within a counting loop, and most languages do this.
2. It is useful to be able to *access the value* of the loop variable outside a counting loop with multiple exits, but few new languages allow this.
3. There is no reason why counting loops should not have *more than one counter*, but we have found only one language which provides this facility (CHILL); or have *no counter* at all.

Turning to conditional loops, we see that there is seldom any explicit identification of the variables involved in the state of the loop. Some of the variables can be discovered in the condition specified with the WHILE or UNTIL, but for multiple-exit loops, any number of other variables may apply. A possible addition to these constructs would be a clause listing the variables, and their initial values. However, it is not immediately clear which variables should be listed. In the WHILE loop of Figure 5.1, i.e.

```
Pascal: i := length(s);
        WHILE (i > 1) and (s[i] <> ' ') do
          i := i - 1;
```

both i and s are mentioned in the condition, but s is not altered within the loop. On the other hand, in the FOR loop example in Figure 5.1 sum and n are altered within the loop, but they are not part of any termination condition. Although forgetting to initialize sum is a very common error in this kind of loop, it would seem that the only feasible qualification for a loop variable should be that it is used in a termination condition and is altered within the loop. Thus, in both examples, only i qualifies as a loop variable.

Can all such loop variables be identified by the compiler? In simple loops, it is merely a matter of detecting variables which are assigned to or used as output parameters (including those from a read or a get). If prospective loop variables are declared outside the procedure in which the loop appears, then a procedure call from within the loop may result in such a variable being altered. Nevertheless, the alteration could still be detected by a compiler employing a simple data flow analysis. A language designer could then decide to extend the requirement for FOR loop variables – that they be declared locally – to all loop variables. This discussion leads straight on to the next element of the control computation.

Initialization

Given the above definition that

> *A loop variable is one that is both checked in a termination condition and is altered during the loop*

it stands to reason that loop variables must be initialized. In most cases, the initialization will be done especially for the loop, i.e. the variables will not just inherit values from previous computations. It would thus add to the understanding of the loop if the initialization appeared in a fixed place before the loop.

Counting loops already have this property, and the idea would be to extend their effect to conditional loops. Following the lead of Algol 68, we permit a FOR clause to appear on its own, which signifies the identification of a loop variable, or with a FROM clause as well, which would enable the variable to be initialized. Taking into account the points made earlier, we shall permit more than one variable to be mentioned, with commas as separators. This use of FOR and FROM differs from that of Algol 68, which has only integer loop variables and does not permit them to be altered in the loop. However, if both a FROM and a TO clause are specified for a loop variable, it would make sense to forbid altering it during the body of the loop. The WHILE loop example of Figure 5.1 then becomes:

```
FOR i FROM length(s)
WHILE (i > 1) and (s[i] <> space) do
  i := i−1;
```

The EXIT WHEN loop of Figure 5.1 is more interesting, as i, ch and s are mentioned in a termination condition and altered in the loop, but only i gets a value especially for the loop. Thus the FROM clause for *ch* and *s* is omitted. Adding to the example, let us suppose that the file may run out of data before either of the other two conditions is met, and that after the loop, if *s* is not full, it must be filled with spaces. This gives:

```
FOR ch, s, input, i FROM first
LOOP
  EXIT WHEN eof(input);
  get(ch);
  EXIT WHEN ch = space;
  s(i) := ch;
  EXIT WHEN i = s'last;
  i := i + 1;
```

```
END LOOP;
FOR i,s
WHILE i < s'last LOOP
  i := i + 1;
  s(i) := space;
END LOOP;
```

(Note that the first part could have been written using a WHILE for eof(input), but we could not have used a counting loop for *i* because then the value of *i* would not have been available in the following part.) Unlike the full form of FOR, the abbreviated FOR FROM does not implicitly define the loop variables, since the type cannot be deduced from thc initialization alone.

The FOR FROM clause could be optional in the following sense. If it is omitted, no identification of loop variables is done. If it is included, all the loop variables are found and all should appear in the FOR; if not, a compilation error occurs, signalling that the programmer has forgotten something. Certainly, even without the compiler recognizing such a clause, it could prove as useful as assertions in reminding the programmer about this essential element of loop control.

Altering loop variables

In endeavouring to identify the essential property of the alteration process, we look at why WHILE loops are used when a FOR loop would be more appropriate. There are two reasons:

1. There is an additional termination condition which will apply before the end of the range of values supplied to the FOR, and the language does not have an EXIT WHEN statement (e.g. Pascal).
2. The alteration required is not a simple step increment or decrement on the previous value (e.g. linked lists or other record values such as dates).

The second reason is the one which sheds the light. Pratt [1978] gives statistics that show that nearly half the loops in the Pascal compiler are concerned with files or lists and that these have to be programmed with WHILEs or REPEATs instead of FORs. In order to accommodate more complex alterations, we need to

- either extend the function of the FOR loop,
- or have a means of identifying stand-alone alterations.

We look first at extending the FOR loop. Apart from Pascal's and Ada's very simple counting up or down facility, three extensions have already been tried in various languages, i.e. step values, discrete lists and element selection.

Several languages (Algol, BASIC, PL/1, CHILL) provide a *step value* so that the loop variable can be altered by a value other than unity. In its full form, the step value may not even be integral. For example,

```
BASIC: FOR X = 0 TO 10 STEP 0.05
```

All language manuals warn of the dangers of such statements because real arithmetic is not exact, and there is a chance that the supposed last alteration would produce 9.9499999, say, causing an unwanted further iteration. In Ada, one would imagine that the effect of the above statement should be achieved by declaring *x* as a fixed point real type, *T*, with a DELTA of 0.05 and then being able to have an implied step with

```
Not Ada: FOR x in T'range LOOP
```

However, this is not allowed.

In Algol 60, a *list of values* could be specified in place of a range, as in

```
Algol 60: FOR i := 0, 1, −1, x*y, x−e do
Algol 60: FOR coin := 0.01, 0.02, 0.05, 0.10, 0.20, 0.50, 1 do
```

The enumerated types of Pascal and Ada approximate this feature as in

```
Ada: TYPE coins is (c1, c2, c5, c10, c20, c50, L1);
     FOR coin in coins do
```

The difficulty is that, by specifying identifiers, the programmer has lost the values and must supply a separate data structure containing these, e.g.

```
Ada: TYPE money is delta 0.01 range 0.0 ..10000000;
     coin_values : array(coins) of money :=
                        (0.01, 0.02, 0.05, 0.10, 0.20, 0.50, 1);
```

Since the number of items in the list is fixed, it would be a small matter for the language to implement the mapping itself, and the Algol 60 feature has much to recommend it. Ada does have the FOR USE representation clause which enables a mapping to be specified, provided the type mapped onto is an integer (an example is given in Section 2.4). This does not help in the coin example.

Finally, we consider *selecting elements of a structure*. This extension is present in the very powerful loop structure in CHILL. In addition to the step and list extensions mentioned above, CHILL permits iteration over an array. The loop variable is given the type of the array's elements and is interpreted as a reference into the elements of the array using the same mechanism as would a call-by-reference parameter. Each alteration presents the next element in the array, under the name of the loop variable.

Compare this to Ada where the variable is of the type of the array's index and the elements are obtained by subsequent indexing. For example:

```
CHILL: DO FOR x in A;
          x := 0;
       OD;
```

with

```
Ada: FOR i in A'range LOOP
        A[i] := 0;
     END LOOP;
```

The CHILL example abstracts completely from the unnecessary detail of the index type and gets straight to the heart of the matter – it is successive elements of A that we want. The Ada attribute facility and implicitly defined loop variable mean that the index type is almost hidden, but the subsequent indexing of A by i is quite unnecessary. Once one has a facility like this, traditional ways of performing loops fall away. For example, even to copy the i+1th element of an array into the ith can be done without dealing in indices, as in

```
CHILL: DO FOR x in A,
              FOR y in A (min+1 : max);
          x := y;
       OD;
       A(max) := 0;
```

Here x is given references to successive values of A starting at A(min) and y is given references to successive values starting at A(min+1). In the statement x:=y, y is dereferenced and its value is assigned to the element referenced by x. This is done until one of the FORs is exhausted, which will be that for y as it has the shorter range. The last element copied would be A(max−1) := A(max). Thus we follow the look with an appropriate assignment into A(max).

It is evident therefore that much has already been done in extending the power of the FOR clause of a loop. What about structures other than arrays? Here we note an essential difference of structures as they relate to iteration. One-dimensional arrays and sequential files have the properties that

- the operation needed to obtain the next element is known to the system, i.e. index plus one;
- there exits a termination condition which is known to the system, i.e. last index in the range for arrays, and end-of-file for a file.

For structures comprising linked nodes, no such conventions exist. The next node is found by means of a pointer field. This field may have any name, appear anywhere in the structure, and may not be unique. Although one usually indicates the end of a list by means of some special pointer value such as nil, this is not mandatory and cannot be relied upon. Therefore a simple extension to FOR is not possible for such structures, although we shall investigate generator-based extensions in the next section.

Checking for termination

A good deal has already been said about termination conditions. In summary we note that

- there can be any number,
- implicit ones appear in FOR and WHILE conditions and are placed at the start of the loop,
- explicit ones should be identified by an EXIT WHEN and they may appear anywhere.

There is no problem with the understanding of these conditions. If multiple FORs are allowed as well as a WHILE, the order in which the conditions are tested must be specified, and that of CHILL seems eminently sensible, i.e. the WHILE is only checked if no FOR terminates.

One aspect of checking is that it is frequently necessary to know outside the loop which of the conditions triggered the end. In the old forms, one simply repeated some of the checks to initiate a follow-up action. Clearly something better can be done.

Follow-up actions

In all the suggestions for new loop constructs, this aspect has received the most consideration. Zahn [1974] first proposed an event-driven control statement which started off with a loop and ended with a case as follows:

```
UNTIL e1 or e2 or ... en do
  loop body
THEN CASE
  e1 : S1;
  e2 : S2;
  ...
  en : Sn;
END;
```

Each of the *ei* are events which, when they occur in the loop body, are indicated by name. Knuth [1974] shows how this construct can be used to solve a simple linear search and gives several other examples, all of which show that events are indeed very useful. However, languages have avoided them and the Ada designers claim that they are unnecessary [Ichbiah *et al.*, 1979] because one can achieve the same effect using the combination of an

IF, an enumerated scalar and an unconditional exit. To illustrate this, we give the string reading example in Zahn's notation and Ada:

```
Zahn: UNTIL ended or aspace or full do
          if eof(input) then ended;
          get(ch);
          if ch = space then aspace;
          s(i) := ch;
          if i = s'last then full;
        THEN CASE
          aspace: UNTIL full do
                      if i = s'last then full;
                      i := i+1;
                      s(i) := space;
                      END;
          full, ended : null;
        END;

Ada: DECLARE
        TYPE state is (ended, aspace, full);
        state : states;
      BEGIN
        LOOP
          if end_of_file then state := ended; exit; end if;
          get(ch);
          if ch = space then state := aspace; exit; end if;
          s(i) := ch;
          if i = s'last then state := full; exit; end if;
          i := i+1;
        END LOOP;
        CASE state of
          WHEN aspace => WHILE i < s'last loop
                             i := i + 1;
                             s(i) := space;
                           END LOOP;
          WHEN others => null;
        END CASE:
      END;
```

Of course, in this example with only one follow-up, the case statement looks out of place, but if we focus on the setting of the events we see that both versions have disadvantages. Both rely on IF statements to check the conditions, whereas the EXIT WHEN was considered an advantage in the control computation. In Zahn's notation, the events seem to be implicitly declared by the UNTIL clause, which raises questions of scope and occlusion for nested loops. Furthermore, the notation is confusing as setting an event looks very like a procedure call, yet control is immediately transferred to the end of the loop. Because of this transfer, ELSE parts are not needed in Zahn's version.

The major disadvantage of the Ada version is that the LOOP and the CASE are separate statements and therefore, if a FOR variable is used, it cannot be referenced in the follow-up. The use of state variables is not of course new, and was discussed in the context of Pascal by Atkinson [1979]. Without the benefit of an exit statement, such loops in Pascal trail off into multiple if–then–else blocks and can become confusing. However, as an aid to the programmer, the state variable approach is probably worth while.

There is a generally held distinction between normal termination and abnormal termination of a loop. Normal termination occurs if the loop completes a FOR clause, i.e. all possible values have been considered; abnormal termination occurs if an EXIT WHEN is obeyed. Bochmann [1973] in an early paper, suggests a similar construct to that of Zahn, but adds that there must be a special event called 'ended' which is signalled upon normal termination. The loop can then be followed by the equivalent of a CASE statement or even an exceptional handler, with the various events listed with corresponding actions.

With the possibility of numerous FORs and a WHILE as well, it is necessary to qualify normal termination. One suggestion is for every termination check, no matter whether explicit or implicit, to identify its event name, when required. Unfortunately, this leads to extra syntax and loops can start to look clumsy. Instead, we retain the idea of normal termination and provide the predefined event ended as suggested by Bochmann, but enable it to be qualified by the loop variable name, e.g. *ended'i*. The WHILE statement, however, cannot indicate an event and would have to be rephrased as an EXIT WHEN. The suggestion for a follow-up facility is as follows.

If a loop requires follow-ups (and not all loops do), all the event names must be listed in the WITH clause along with the loop variables. Those termination conditions that will result in a follow-up (and not all will) then indicate their appropriate event name between the EXIT and the WHEN. If normal termination occurs (i.e. a FOR clause is completed) the event *ended'x* is raised, where *x* is the name of the loop variable. If abnormal termination occurs and an event is specified, then it is raised, otherwise no event is raised and the loop terminates completely. If an event is raised, control transfers to the list of WHEN clauses at the end of the loop and the appropriate one is executed. In the case of the ended event, the value of the loop variable mentioned is undefined, but otherwise it can be used freely. The reading string example is now rewritten as:

```
FOR ch, s, input, EVENT outofdata, i IN s'range
LOOP
   EXIT outofdata WHEN eof(input);
   get(ch);
   EXIT outofdata WHEN ch = space;
   s(i) := ch;
WHEN outofdata =>
```

```
    FOR i in i+1..s'last
    LOOP
      s(i) := space;
    END LOOP;
  END LOOP;
```

Note that *i* can now be controlled by a counting loop as it will still be in scope when the follow-up is performed.

A different approach to follow-ups is taken by Alphard. The designers argue that in most cases only one follow-up is needed, and they provide this as part of a FIRST–SUCHTHAT–THEN–ELSE construct. The FIRST clause is similar to a FOR clause and the SUCHTHAT specifies all the abnormal termination conditions. If one of the latter occurs, the THEN part is executed; otherwise the range of values has been exhausted and the ELSE part is executed. An important refinement is that the loop variable specified in FIRST is available in the THEN part, but not in the ELSE part where it would be undefined. The reading string example can be neatly written in Alphard as:

```
Alphard: i:=1;
         FIRST ch in get(input)
           SUCHTHAT ch = space or eof(input)
             s(i) := ch;
             i := i + 1;
         THEN FOR i : upto(i+1,max) DO
           s(i) := space;
         ELSE null;
```

The main loop is based on the generation of characters, not on the string's index, since the termination conditions refer to the data. For simple cases, this is a useful construct.

5.3 Generators

We now extend the power of iterators by coupling them with generators. In essence, a generator will specify the control computation for a loop, while the iterator will retain the control flow. The previous section introduced various improvements aimed at enhancing the understanding of traditional loop constructs. Most progress was made in the following three areas:

- the identity and initializing of loop variables for WHILE loops;
- the number and type of loop variables for FOR loops;
- the provision of suitable follow-up clauses.

What remains to be done is the extension of FOR loops to data structures that have next operations and termination conditions that cannot be specified simply or implied. The archetype of such structures is a linked list of records. There are many ways of specifying linked lists, but we shall assume that the list consists of nodes; each node has a single link; there is an empty header node that points to the first real node; and that there are three list pointers called front, back and current which react appropriately.

Suppose we wished to use such a structure to:

1. set up a list of public holidays that are read in;
2. write out the contents of the list;
3. find the first public holiday after 1 July.

We would start by ensuring that we can suitably manipulate the type of item in the nodes, i.e. dates. This requirement is satisfied by a separate package called dater which has subprograms to read, write and compare dates. Then the Ada program to set up the list and search it is given in Figure 5.2.

The second two segments involve scanning the list, and the statements to set this up and achieve it have to be repeated in each case. To emphasize this point, here are those statements, with the body of the loop removed.

```
Ada: -- scanning a list
     IF list.front /= list.back then          -- check for empty
        list.current := list.front.link;      -- initialize
        WHILE list.current /= null LOOP       -- termination condition
           .....                              -- loop body
        END LOOP;                             -- altering
     END IF;
```

In exactly the same way, we can identify the loop computation elements of a loop to scan an array with n elements present, i.e.

```
Ada: --- scanning an array
     IF n/= a'first THEN                      -- check for empty
        i := a'first;                         -- initialize
        WHILE i /= n LOOP                     -- termination condition
           ...                                -- loop body
           i := i + 1;                        -- altering
        END LOOP;
     END IF;
```

The pattern of iteration remains the same, only the details of the computation change, and these rely on the data type being iterated over. Therefore we should be able to separate out these details from the loop, and define them at the place where the type itself is defined.

Generators in Alphard

Let us look at such a scheme which has been implemented in Alphard [Shaw *et al.*, 1977]. They define the meaning of a loop in three parts:

```
WITH text_io,dater;  USE text_io,dater;

PROCEDURE test_lists is

    TYPE nodes;
    TYPE tonodes is access nodes;
    TYPE nodes   is record
           link : tonodes;
           data : dates;
         END record;
    TYPE lists   is record
           front,
           back,
           current : tonodes;
         END record;
    list : lists;
  cutoff : constant dates := (1,7,1986);

  BEGIN
    list.front := NEW nodes;
    list.front.link := null;
    list.back := list.front;
    list.current := list.front;
    FOR i in 1..10 LOOP
      list.current.link := NEW nodes;
      list.current := list.current.link;
      list.back := list.current;
      get (list.current.data);
    END LOOP;

    IF list.front /= list.back then
      list.current := list.front.link;
      WHILE list.current /= null loop
        put(list.current.data);
        list.current := list.current.link;
      END LOOP;
    END IF;

    IF list.front /= list.back then
      list.current := list.front.link;
      WHILE list.current /= null loop
        EXIT WHEN list.current.data > cutoff;
        list.current := list.current.link;
      END LOOP;
      put(cutoff);
      IF list.current /= null
        THEN put_line(" Found");
        ELSE put_line (" Not found");
      END IF;
    END IF;
  END test_lists;
```

Figure 5.2 List loops in Ada

1. the *iterator*, which gives the syntax and broad semantics, supplied by the language (this would be our control flow);
2. the *generator*, which gives the details of loop control, supplied by the abstraction that is controlling the iteration (our control computation);
3. the *loop body*, supplied by the user.

Alphard provides two iterators, called FOR and FIRST, which serve as templates and must be specialized by information supplied by a generator.

The generator must define two functions called &init and &next which can be invoked by the iterator to produce a sequence of values to bind the loop variable. In general, a generator is a separate form from that in which the data type is defined, and it is said to extend the type. Thus one could have several generators for a given type, permitting different kinds of iteration. Figure 5.3 shows the equivalent Alphard code to that of Figure 5.2. (We assume that pointers are initialized to nil on creation.)

There are two generators, both of which extend a previously defined form called lists which defines a list type such as that in the Ada example. Maker can be used when constructing a list as it continuously returns new empty nodes. Notice that the boolean values of maker's &init and &next functions are always true, since there is no occasion for them to terminate

```
FORM maker EXTENDS L : lists =
  BEGINFORM
  SPECIFICATIONS
    &init (M : maker) RETURNS b:boolean;
    &next (M : maker) RETURNS b:boolean;
  IMPLEMENTATION
    BODY &init = (alloc(M.L.front);
                  M.L.back ← M.L.front;
                  M.L.current ← M.L.front;
                  b ← true);
    BODY &next = (alloc(M.L.current.link);
                   M.L.current ← M.L.current.link;
                   M.L.back ← M.L.current;
                   b ← true);
  ENDFORM;

FORM scanner EXTENDS L : lists =
  BEGINFORM
  SPECIFICATIONS
    &init (S : scanner) RETURNS b:boolean;
    &next (S : scanner) RETURNS b:boolean;
  IMPLEMENTATION
    BODY &init = (b ← S.L.front <> S.L.back;
                  S.L.current ← S.L.front.link);
    BODY &next = (S.L.current ← S.L.current.link;
                   b ← S.L.current <> nil);
  ENDFORM

LOCAL list : lists;

FOR list : maker WHILE not eof DO get(list.current.date);

FOR list : scanner DO put(list.current.date);

FIRST list : scanner SUCHTHAT list.current.date > (1,7,year)
  THEN put (list.current.date)
  ELSE put ('No public holidays after 1 July');
```

Figure 5.3 Loops in Alphard using generators

the loop. On the other hand, scanner – which can be used for scanning through a loop – does have termination conditions built into these functions. Forms are essentially abstract data types and only define a concept. It is necessary to create instances of the concept by means of, say, a local statement, e.g. LOCAL list : lists;.

The semantics are exactly those of the equivalent Ada code. In the searching example, when the FIRST statement begins, scanner's &init function is called which tests for an empty list and in any case sets current to front.link. If &init returns false (i.e. the list is empty) then the ELSE part is executed immediately. If nodes do exist then the SUCHTHAT clause is evaluated. If no match is found, scanner is called again, this time for its &next function. This moves current on and then checks to see if the end of the list has been reached. So once again, FIRST may terminate and pass control to the ELSE.

A further abstraction

The importance of generators such as these is that they can be re-used for many loops. Thus the intricate code for scanning the loop is written once and once only. This is the story of procedures all over again, but at this level we would call it data abstraction. We now consider whether we have used the generator facility fully. In all three loops, we refer to list.current.date; that is, we want the date, but we still have to know that it is stored in a list accessed by the pointer called current. Would it be possible to hide this detail by having the generator return dates rather than lists? In other words, the list would be local to a new generator which would return only the date field each time it was activated, rather than a list header, as at present. This is certainly possible, provided that &init and &next can be called explicitly and that they can return values in their parameters. Although it is unlikely that Alphard would allow these liberties, we can still pursue the idea. We define two new generators which extend types dates and connect them in some way to those for lists. This is shown in Figure 5.4.

We must now carefully consider what is happening here. When the statement

```
FIRST holiday: datescanner (list) ...
```

is executed, a loop variable called *holiday* of type *pointer to date* is set up, in the same way as in CHILL's loop construct. We see this as the formal name of a var parameter. The actual name is supplied by the generator each time it is called. In *datescanner* this is *D*. The value supplied to *D* is that obtained from *L.current.date*, where *L* is the formal name for the local variable, *list*, in the generator. *L* obtains its values in a straight function call to one of the *listscanner*'s functions.

In assessing this abstraction, one feels positive towards the iterators. For example, to do the same for public holidays for France, say, one would only need to write

```
LOCAL Frenchpublics : lists;

FOR holiday : datemaker (Frenchpublics)
  WHILE not eof DO get (holiday);

FOR holiday: datescanner(Frenchpublics) DO put(holiday);

FIRST holiday : datescanner(Frenchpublics)
  SUCHTHAT holiday > (1,7,year)
  THEN put(holiday)
  ELSE put ('No public holidays after 1 July');
```

However, one's instinct warns against the complexity of the generators. This complexity is not in the statements needed, which are few and simple, but in

```
FORM datemaker(VAR L : lists) EXTENDS D : dates;
  USES listmaker;
  BEGINFORM
  SPECIFICATIONS
    &init (D : datemaker) RETURNS b : boolean;
    &next (M : datemaker) RETURNS b : boolean;
  IMPLEMENTATION
    BODY &init = (b ← listmaker.&init(L);
                  D ← L.current.date);
         &next = (b ← listmaker.&next(L);
                  D ← L.current.date);
  ENDFORM;
FORM datescanner (VAR L : lists) EXTENDS D : dates;
  USES listmaker;
  BEGINFORM
  SPECIFICATIONS
    &init (D : datescanner) RETURNS b : boolean;
    &next (D : datescanner) RETURNS b : boolean;
  IMPLEMENTATION
    BODY &init = (b ← listmaker.&init (L);
                  if b then D ← L.current.date);
         &next = (b ← listmaker.&next (L);
                  if b then D ← L.current.date);
  ENDFORM;
  LOCAL holiday : dates; list : lists;
  FOR holiday : datemaker(list) WHILE not eof DO get(holiday);
  FOR holiday : datescanner(list) DO put(holiday);
  FIRST holiday : datescanner(list) SUCHTHAT holiday > (1,7,year)
    THEN put (holiday)
    ELSE put ('No public holidays after 1 July');
```

Figure 5.4 An attempt at generalizing generators

the interaction between the various objects as parameters to forms and functions. In this example, a great deal of the protection against mistakes would be achieved by the type checking mechanism so that lists and dates could not be confused. However, if the various levels of forms were based on the same type, such as integer, it would not be as easy to write the generators correctly. With the intention being that generators would be written rarely, and then once and for all, the complexity can perhaps be accepted, because the gains are certainly great. Woitok [1983] investigated this same problem and came to the conclusion that, apart from generics, one also needed incremental record definitions so that the link fields could be defined apart from the data. His suggestion has been implemented in a systems programming language, ALICE.

We note again that, in any case, the code of Figure 5.4 is hypothetical, as it relies on side-effects and other non-Alphard features. In the next section we look at the extent to which these ideas can be implemented in Ada.

5.4 Iterators and generators in Ada

> The iteration statement is the most important point of interaction between data and the control structure of the language itself. [Shaw *et al.*, 1977]

Ada has only a primitive loop control construct, but its powerful data abstraction facilities should enable other iterators to be defined which will be independent of the data structure and rely on generic packages serving as generators. Experience with defining such a package for a general searching loop has shown up some blind spots in Ada's data abstraction facilities, and ways of getting around these are discussed. But first we examine the simple iteration facilities provided by Ada.

Iteration in Ada

In Section 4.2, a package to read and write a table of items was developed (Figure 4.1). We can now make several more comments about the level of abstraction that can be achieved with Ada's iteration features and the design of the loop in general.

1. *Protected range.* The loop variable, `i`, is defined on the exact range of the array and the altering statement, `i:=succ(i)`, is guarded against the last case. The same guard is then used as entry to the follow-up loop. The importance of this guard cannot be overestimated: even the most experienced programmers have been known to omit it, presumably for the sake of simplicity of expression [Sale, 1981].
2. *State variable.* It is very likely that one of the termination conditions will coincide with that needed to guard the altering statement. Instead of

repeating the question, the answer is calculated once and stored in a state variable. Not only is less work done, but the correctness of the order of the checks can be more easily established. Moreover, if more terminating conditions are necessary, the loops without state variables become decidely hard to read. (A full discussion of the use of state variables is given in Atkinson [1979].)

3. *Starting outside the range*. One defect in the iterator as presented is that it does not cope with the case of no input. For example, suppose the routines are used to read in strings where a blank terminates the input. It is perfectly possible that a null line of input may be supplied, in which case the table (or string) should be filled with blanks by the follow-up loop. There are two ways of handling this case. A simple IF over the first loop would do the trick, or another solution is to make both loops have the incrementation in the beginning and start the loop parameter outside the range.

This latter technique is used by Pascal programmers, who habitually declare two types for an array's domain, i.e.

```
Pascal: tablerange = 1..max;
        tableindex = 0..max;
```

and use loops such as

```
Pascal: i := 0;
        if not eof {or whatever} then
        repeat
          i := succ(i);
          read(table[i]);
          if table[i] = itemender then state := ended else
          if       i = max        then state := filled;
        until state <> reading;
        while state <> filled do begin
          i := succ(i);
          table[i] := itemender;
          if i = max then state := filled
        end;
```

In the opinion of the author, this makes for much clearer control computation but the equivalent data types are very difficult to define in Ada. Firstly, there does not exist a common equivalent to 0 for the other discrete types (character and enumerated). Secondly, in Ada, defining the two connected types, boundindex and boundrange, is very difficult. Boundindex is an extension of the range, and so cannot be a subtype, and there is no mechanism for deriving a new type by simply hitching a new value on. As has been shown, the use of extra values can be avoided by deft programming, but the author is not sure that the language should force these guards. Perhaps there should exist pred(range'first) and succ(range'last)

with appropriate rules governing their use. There is a good treatise on the further implications of unassigned objects in Winner [1984].

Machine implications

There are some thought-provoking implications for machine design here. If the accepted way of programming loops is to declare the index over exactly the array's range and to guard the incrementation against the last case, then a very similar pattern should exist at the machine level. However, most code generators do not do this and a FOR loop is typically implemented as

```
Ada: i := first;
     WHILE i <= last LOOP
       -- code for statement
       i := succ(i);
     END LOOP;
```

rather than

```
Ada: i := first;
     IF i <= last then
       LOOP
         -- code for statement
         exit when i = last;
         i := succ(i);
       END LOOP
     END IF;
```

If subranges are represented at machine level, as has been proposed in Bishop [1980], then the first extract would not be valid, unless an internal copy of i with the extended bounds is used instead. Since the loop parameter in Ada is meant to be an 'internal copy' anyway, there does not seem to be any justification for such subterfuge.

It is notable that the Pascal Report avoids defining the FOR loop to act as in the first extract (although the Algol 60 Report does), and subsequent language definitions have followed suit. In Pascal, the FOR loop is defined as a sequence of the body statement expanded out as many times as necessary, and in Euclid the definition makes use of the generator for the data type, which presumably applies or does not apply the guard as it sees fit. Ada's description is a combination of these, i.e. the loop variables take each of the values of the given discrete range in turn.

A generalized searching loop

Pratt's figures [Pratt, 1978] indicate that a double-exit searching loop is a common standard pattern in system programs. This is borne out by a count done of the disk controller section of the Juniper operating system [Mitchell, private communication] which has 20% of all loops in this category. As we have seen, Alphard provides this facility with its FIRST template. For example, to search A for a given value x and add it on if not there, we have

```
Alphard: first i : upto (1,n) suchthat A[i] = x
         then write ('Duplicate')
         else begin
            n := n+1;
            A[n] := x;
         end;
```

This very powerful construct combines a neat control flow mechanism with the abstraction facility of the generator. Matching the control flow can actually be achieved by means of a function in a language like Pascal, although the strict typing means different versions of the function for different types. In Ada, much can be done in making the loop generic, but the control flow is quite different.

The control flow

As a first try, we envisage a boolean function with the loop variable and the suchthat clause as parameters. The call would then look something like

```
IF thereexists (an => i, suchthat => a[i] = x, until => n)
   then put ('Duplicate');
   else
      n := n + 1;
      a(n) := x;
END IF;
```

The value of such a function is in the amount of control computation that can be hidden from the user. This is illustrated in the version of the function implemented in Pascal, shown in Figure 5.5. Packaging the loop up in this function relieves the user of having to refer to the words *found* or *notthere*, which after all were part of the searching mechanism and not really part of the problem being solved. Notice that the table, *a*, is not a parameter to the function. Since it has to be accessed globally by the condition function, it may as well be accessed globally by *thereexists* as well. The advantage is that the search can then be applied to a table with any type of components, provided it is defined over the same range.

We find, however, that it is not possible to set up an identical control structure in Ada. The features which are lacking are:

1. *Call-by-name*. It is a truism that call-by-name is a most unappreciated parameter passing mechanism. The reason seems to stem from a belief

```
{Definitions needed outside the function thereexists}
CONST max = ...;
TYPE index = 0..max;
     range = 1..max;
     table = array [range] of thing;
FUNCTION thereexists     (var        i           : index;
                                     n           : index;
                          var        start       : index;
                          function   condition   (i : index)
                                                 : boolean) : boolean;
  VAR state : (searching, found, notthere);
  BEGIN
    i := start;
    state := searching;
    if i > n then state := notthere else
    repeat
      if condition(i) then state := found else
      if i = n        then state := notthere
                      else i := succ(i);
    until state <> searching;
    case state of
      found    : thereexists := true;
      notthere : thereexists := false;
    end; {case}
    start := i;
END; {thereexists}
```

Figure 5.5 An array searching function in Pascal

that there are not any real algorithms for which call-by-name is necessary (Jensen's device is for academics!) and a horror of aliasing and inefficiency [Brosgol, 1984]. An iterator graphically illustrates its forte: if a subprogram contains a loop with a termination condition which must be evaluated for successive values of the loop index, the rule for this evaluation must be passed as a parameter. If the rule itself cannot be passed, a second best is the name of the rule, as in Pascal's formal procedure mechanism. Without any facility to pass a rule, the iterator has to be turned inside out, with the loop around the call itself. The successive evaluation of the condition is done outside the iterator and passed as a boolean parameter. The work of the iterator is thus considerably reduced, but it still performs checks in the correct order, returns the appropriate value of i and has two exit points.

2. *Call-by-reference in a function*. Ada does not permit output parameters in functions. Thus thereexists cannot be a function; in order to update the value of the index, it must be a procedure. Therefore the result of the search cannot be used directly by an IF–THEN–ELSE, but has to be transmitted explicitly in some other way. Various solutions present themselves. One way is to include a result parameter and follow the

loop by a case statement. This has the advantage of being extensible to several result values. Alternatively, exceptions can be raised. These would be defined in the package containing the iterator. In order for the exceptions to halt the loop, the loop and the handlers must be included in a block. If we have to use a block, then we can take advantage of it and declare the index as local to the loop. We now have

```
Ada: DECLARE i : a'range; begin
        LOOP
          forfirst (i, suchthat => a[i] = x, until => n);
        END LOOP; exception
        WHEN found => put ('Duplicate');
        WHEN notthere =>
                n := n + 1;
                a(n) := x;
        END;
```

```
GENERIC
  TYPE index is private;
  initial,
  final        : in index;
  WITH FUNCTION next (i : index) return index is index'succ;

  PACKAGE search is
    PROCEDURE forfirst (an        : out index;
                        suchthat  : boolean;
                        from      : index := initial;
                        until     : index := final);
    found, notthere : exception;
  END search;

  PACKAGE BODY search is
    TYPE states is (setup, searching, gotit, exhausted);
    current,
    ender       : index;
    state       : states := setup;
    PROCEDURE forfirst (an        : out index;
                        suchthat  : boolean;
                        from      : index := initial;
                        until     : index := final) is
      BEGIN
        IF state = setup then
           state := searching;
           current := from;
           ender := until;
        END if;

        IF state = searching then
           IF suchthat then state:=gotit;
              elsif current = ender then state := exhausted;
                                     else current := next(current);
           END IF;
           an := current;
        END if;

        CASE state is
           WHEN gotit    => state := setup; RAISE found;
           WHEN exhausted=> state := setup; RAISE notthere;
           WHEN setup|searching=> null ;
        END case;
      END forfirst;
    END search;
```

Figure 5.6 A generic iterator in Ada

The control computation

Despite the fact that the above structure is not as neat as Alphard's or even Pascal's, once the procedure is made generic, a considerable saving in effort can be realized. Figure 5.6 gives the full Ada package to perform the loop.

Examples of instantiations and uses of the package are:

1. *Array search.* In the simple case, the default for the next routine can be invoked but the initial and final values, which will be defaults when the procedure is called, must still be indicated. Figure 5.7 shows such an instantiation and its use in setting up a table of unique values. The example makes good use of keyword parameters and initialization.
2. *Date search.* As the control computation becomes more complex, we use a package as a generator for the iterator package (Figure 5.8). In fact, the iterator can be instantiated inside the generator, thus increasing the operations made available for the type. Notice that, in this example, no array or sequence is involved in the search: the generator is simply providing values from a function.

```
WITH text_io, search;  USE text_io;

PROCEDURE iterator is

  TYPE     real        is digits 6;
  TYPE     vector      is array(1..10) of real;
  SUBTYPE  vectorrange is integer range vector'range;
  PACKAGE  real_io     is new float_io(real); use real_io;

  PACKAGE search_vector is new search (vectorrange,
                                       vector'first,
                                       vector'last);
  USE search_vector;

  v : vector;
  n : integer range vector'range := vector'first;
  x : real;

  BEGIN
    get(v(1));
    LOOP
      get(x); put(x);
      search : declare i : integer range vector'range:=vector'first;
        BEGIN LOOP
            search_vector.forfirst(i, suchthat => v(i)=x, until => n);
        END loop;
        EXCEPTION
        WHEN found     => put (" Duplicate");
        WHEN notthere => n := integer'succ(n);
                         v(n) := x;
      END search;
      new_line;
      EXIT when n = v'last;
    END loop;
  END iterator;
```

Figure 5.7 Example of using an iterator

Assessment

This investigation has shown that the level of abstraction that can be achieved for iterations is slightly limited on the side of control flow, but fairly good in control computation.

```
PACKAGE datetheory is
  TYPE date is -- the usual;
  PROCEDURE get (d : out dates);
  PROCEDURE swopdates (d1,d2 : in out dates) is new
                        exchange(dates);
  FUNCTION nextweekday is (d : dates) returns dates;
  FUNCTION "+" (d : dates; day : days) returns boolean;
  dayone : constant dates := (1,1,thisyear);
  today : dates;
  yearend: constant dates := (31,12,thisyear);
  PACKAGE scandates is new search (dates, dayone, yearend,
nextweekday);
  USE scandates;
END datetheory;
USE datetheory, timetheory; -- which has been similarly defined
PROCEDURE appointment;
  thistime : times;
  FUNCTION freeat (t : time) return boolean;
    -- Consults a diary. Define it later;
  PROCEDURE book (d : dates, t : time);
    -- Updates a diary. Define it later;
  BEGIN
    get (thistime);
    DECLARE weekday : dates := today begin
      LOOP
        forfirst (weekday, until => today + 3,
                  suchthat => freeat (thistime));
      END LOOP; exception
      when found => put ('OK That's fine');
                    book (weekday, thistime);
      WHEN notthere => put ('Sorry. Can I try another time?');
    END;
  END appointment;
```

Figure 5.8 Example of using an iterator for dates

The control flow of the general search loop is different to Pascal's because of the lack of procedure parameters or call-by-name and the restriction against side-effects in functions. However, it may well be that the resulting structure, consisting as it does of a block, a loop and a list of exception handlers, may become more acceptable to programmers as they develop their styles in Ada. In particular, programming with exceptions will produce a quite different style to that of the goto-less Pascal school. On the other hand, it can be argued that having the loop at the point of call spoils the abstraction of the search and that the lack of procedure parameters is a serious drawback in Ada.

There are several features of Ada that contribute towards the clarity of expression achieved when calling an iterator, and the level of generality in the iterator itself. These are keyword parameters, parameter defaults, generic procedure defaults and attributes. Like other Ada features, e.g. overloading, there is of course no way in which the language can check that a generator works as an iterator expects. This will have to be done by convention, and will rely heavily on the specification of the iterator being completely clear. By defining iterators in a uniform way, and ensuring that they do in fact take care of all boundary conditions, the chances of error will be minimized.

Exercises

1. Pratt [1978] stated that 'A central element in understanding a loop is the determination of the control flow and control computation'. Discuss this statement by defining the notions of control flow and control computation, and by evaluating the degree of understanding which is evident in the loops of existing languages.
2. Shaw *et al.* [1977] stated that 'The iteration statement is the most important point of interaction between data and the control structure of the language itself'. Discuss how this interaction is provided by Alphard forms, showing how Alphard achieves both ease of use and verifiable protection from misuse, illustrating your answer by means of examples where necessary.
3. Ada does not support procedure parameters. In order to achieve the abstraction of iterators and generators, other Ada features must be used. Two suggestions are *generic packages* and *tasks* [Lamb and Hilfinger, 1983]. Describe these two approaches, using examples, and evaluate their relative effectiveness and ease of use.
4. Discuss the rationale behind the varying approaches taken by languages in protecting FOR loop variables.

References

Atkinson, LV., 1979. 'Pascal scalars as state indicators', *SPE*, **9(6)**, 427–432.

Bishop, J.M., 1980. 'Effective machine descriptors for Ada', Proceedings of the Ada Symposium. In *SIGPLAN*, **15(11)**, 235–242.

Bochmann, G.V., 1973. 'Multiple exits from a loop without the GOTO', *CACM*, **16(7)**, 443–444.

Bohm, C. and Jacopini, G., 1966. 'Flow diagrams, Turing Machines and languages with only two transformation rules', *CACM*, **9(5)**, 366–371.

Brosgol, B., 1984. 'Ada implementation notes – passing subprograms as parameters', *Ada Letters*, **III(6)**, 118–120.

Ichbiah, J.D., Heliard, J.C., Roubine, O., Barnes, J.G.P., Krieg-Bruckner, B. and Wickmann, B.A., 1979. 'Rationale for the design of the Ada programming language', *SIGPLAN*, **14(6)**, Part B.

Knuth, D.E., 1974. 'Structured programming with go to statements', *Computing Surveys*, **6(4)**, 261–301.

Lamb, D.A. and Hilfinger, P.N., 1983. 'Simulation of procedure variables using Ada tasks', *IEEE-SE*, **9(1)**, 13–15.

Pratt, T.W., 1978. 'Control computations and the design of loop control structures', *IEEE-SE*, **4(2)**, 81–89.

Sale, A.J.H., 1981. 'Proposal for extension to Pascal', *SIGPLAN*, **16(4)**, 98–103.

Shaw, M., Wulf, W.A. and London, R.L., 1977. 'Abstraction and verification in Alphard – defining and specifying iteration and generators', *CACM*, **20(8)**, 553–564.

Winner, R.I., 1984. 'Unassigned objects', *TOPLAS*, **6(4)**, 449–67.

Woitok, R., 1983. 'Abstracting linked data structures using incremental records', *SIGPLAN*, **18(11)**, 54–63.

Zahn, C.T., 1974. 'A control statement for natural top-down structured programming', *Programming Symposium: Proceedings, Colloquia sur la programmation*, Paris, April 1974, Springer-Verlag.

Chapter 6 Abstractions for Concurrency

The main thrust of data abstraction in programming languages has always been towards improving the quality of sequential programming, with the needs of concurrent systems being catered for by low level primitives. The steady, innovative work of Dijkstra, Hoare, Brinch Hansen and others in applying abstraction to the problems of concurrency has resulted in modern languages now being equipped with powerful concurrent features. In this chapter we look at the evolution of abstraction facilities for concurrency, from the primitive semaphore to the powerful rendezvous. The emphasis is on the languages features and the issues raised in using them effectively, rather than on their applications in real-time systems.

6.1 What is concurrency?

A program can be viewed as consisting of one or more *processes*, each of which consists of statements which are executed *sequentially*. When there are two or more processes, they may be specified as executing at the same time, or *concurrently*. Concurrency is therefore the notion of simultaneous execution of sequential processes.

To be effective, these processes would need to *communicate* information and to *synchronize* actions that depend on each other. The basis for both these activities would be certain shared data, where communication would involve the value of the data and synchronization would depend on its state, for example whether it was there or not.

On top of the concurrency of a program, there may be time constraints on execution introduced by the outside world, such as required responses to physical devices. Programs with time constraints are known as *real-time* programs, although for a time this term was used interchangeably with 'concurrent'. Wirth [1977a] gives a very clear discussion on the difference.

A concurrent program may be executed on a variety of *processor* configurations, giving rise to the following terms:

- *multiprogramming*: the processes share the processor, only one executing at a time;
- *multiprocessing*: the processes run on their own processors, sharing a common memory;

- *distributed processing*: the processes run on their own processors, connected by a communications network.

The configurations should not affect the operation of the concurrent features used, although some will be more suited to the distributed approach then others, as we shall see.

The swing away from assembly language which gained genuine momentum during the seventies was slow to affect the area of concurrent systems – operating systems, embedded control systems and the like. What happened was that three people – Edsger Dijkstra, Tony Hoare and Per Brinch Hansen – independently developed key abstractions which were taken up by researchers worldwide, realized in experimental languages, reported on, adapted and refined. In this way, the problems of concurrency could be expressed in well understood notations, and solutions and principles gradually evolved. We can therefore distinguish between these abstractions, the features used to realize them in a given language and the method finally used to implement the concurrency on the hardware provided.

The features that began to be provided in the late 1970s were, in the main, integrated into the general abstraction mechanism of the language and all along the issue of verifying programs using them was considered. The whole quest was to improve reliability, as Wortmann [1977] says:

> Reliability is not something that can be added to a language by *post hoc* changes. In particular, additions to a language are more likely to increase reliability problems that to solve them. What is ultimately required is a new generation of languages designed for reliable software.

It is evident that the realm of concurrency is now firmly within the ambit of reliable languages and that future designs will provide for concurrent processing as a matter of course.

However, we still have more than one key abstraction and although a hierarchy is identifiable there is no clear indication that any one approach will stand alone in the future. We must therefore look at all the proposals, how they evolved, their advantages, disadvantages and optimal areas of application. One helpful aspect is that the literature on concurrency includes a number of recent survey papers comparing the abstractions and features currently available. The most valuable papers are those by Welsh and Lister [1981], Stotts [1982] and Andrews and Schneider [1983]. These papers form the basis for the material presented in the next section.

6.2 Concurrency constructs

In the beginning, processes were simply sequences of instructions, not delineated in any way, and they achieved synchronization by setting and testing ordinary variables. The testing was done repeatedly until the variable acquired the correct value, and so these variables came to be known as *spin-*

locks. The problem was that the spinning occupied the processor, yet interrupts could still occur in the middle of a set or test, with unpredictable results.

Dijkstra [1968] in a milestone paper called 'Cooperating sequential processes' made a radical improvement by defining these variables as *semaphores*. A semaphore is a non-negative integer on which the set and test operations are defined, and these are guaranteed to be indivisible. That is to say that interrupts are not allowed while semaphores are being manipulated. The set operation (or *V*) increments a semaphore and the test (or *P*) delays until it is possible to decrement it. Although not touted as such, this definition of a semaphore is precisely that of an abstract data type, and is probably the first such to become widely accepted and used. Using the notation of Chapter 2, we could define it as

```
TYPE semaphore
  DEFINITION
    integer range 0..maxint;
  OPERATIONS
    P (semaphore); INDIVISIBLE;
    V (semaphore); INDIVISIBLE;
  IMPLEMENTATION
   PROCEDURE P (var s : semaphore);
      begin
        while s = 0 do delay;
        s := s-1;
      end; {P}
    PROCEDURE V (var s : semaphore);
      begin
        s := s+1;
      end; {V}
  END semaphore;
```

The beauty of semaphores is their simplicity. Provided one can guarantee that the *P* and *V* operations will not be interrupted, semaphores can be implemented in any language and system. Yet, with just these simple primitives, effective synchronization can be achieved.

The synchronization problems

In working with semaphores, it became clear that there were two distinct synchronization problems:

- *selective mutual exclusion* when two processes sharing the same data must access it separately;
- *conditional synchronization* when a process needs to wait until shared data is in the correct state.

In each case, one associates a semaphore with the data and then observes a protocol of calls on *P* and *V*. In the case of mutual exclusion, the *P* and *V* are done on either side of the statements accessing the shared data, as in

```
P(sem);      {gain access}
  critical section
V(sem);      {relinquish control}
```

For conditional synchronization, one process (known as the producer for that particular data area) issues a *V* indicating that the data is ready, while another process (the consumer) issues a *P* just before it needs to use the data. In this way, the consumer is blocked until the producer has done its job. Viewed the other way, the producer should not proceed to produce another set of values for the data until the consumer has removed the first. Therefore, two semaphores are used and the protocol would be:

```
producer: P(empty);           {wait until empty}
            P(sem);
              produce values
            V(sem);
          V(full);            {indicate full}
consumer: P(full);            {wait until full}
            P(sem);
              consume values
            V(sem);
          V(empty);           {indicate empty}
```

There is a definite symmetry about the use of semaphores, but once programs extend beyond a page, the *P*s and *V*s become unconnected and it is very hard to ensure that they match up and are in the right place. Perhaps the most severe drawback of semaphores, though, is that their association with particular data areas is not explicitly specified or controlled. The programmer must rely entirely on good variable names, comments and conventions to convey what is actually happening.

Higher level constructs

It was evident that these solutions to the synchronization problems could be expressed at a higher level. Over the ten years from Dijkstra's first paper, three major concepts were defined, mainly through the work of Hoare [1972, 1974, 1978] and Brinch Hansen [1973, 1978]. These are

- conditional critical regions,
- monitors,
- message passing.

From these, Ada's powerful rendezvous facility emerged, as shown in Figure 6.1. (The arrows indicate historical as well as conceptual relationships.)

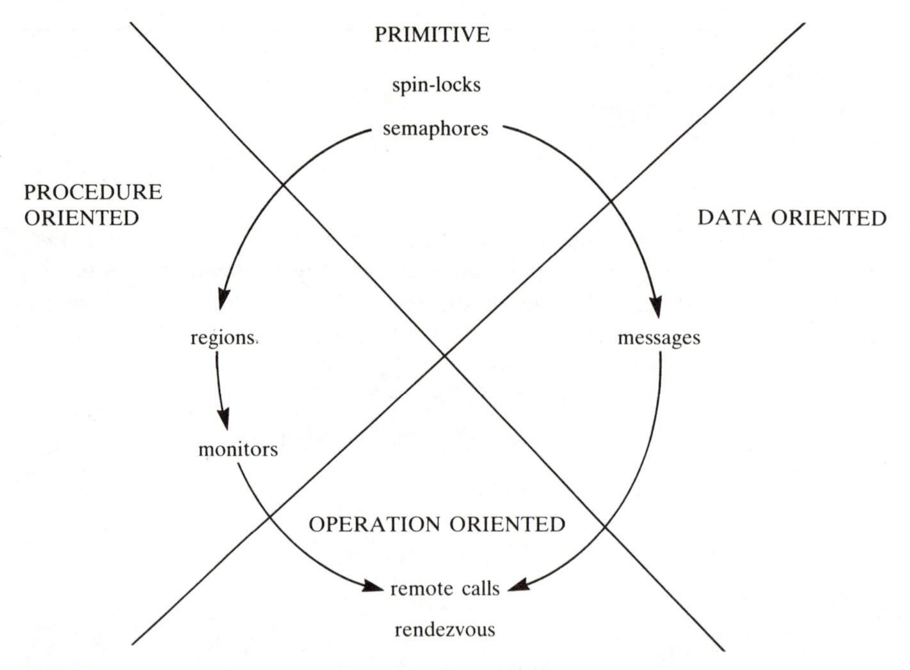

Figure 6.1 Evolution of concurrent concepts (adapted from Andrews and Schneider [1983])

In this section we describe each of these abstractions briefly and then go on in the next section to discuss them under language issues and to look at the variations in languages that use them.

Conditional critical regions

Conditional critical regions were a first attempt at abstracting away from semaphores. Each group of shared data is called a *resource*. The critical sections within each process are designated as *regions* and each region mentions the resources that it accesses. It is then guaranteed that two regions referring to the same resource will not be active simultaneously. Hence mutual exclusion is assured. To achieve synchronization based on the state of a resource, conditions may be attached to the start of a region. For example, a simple producer and consumer using a string buffer could be expressed as:

```
RESOURCE buffer
  DEFINITION
    string := '';
  END buffer;
PROCESS producer;
  VAR s : string;
  BEGIN
    loop
      create values in s;
      REGION buffer WHEN length(buffer) = 0
        buffer := s;
      END region;
    end loop;
  END; {producer}
PROCESS consumer;
  VAR s : string;
  BEGIN
    loop
      REGION buffer WHEN length(buffer) > 0
        s := buffer;
        buffer := ' ';
      END region;
      do something with s;
    end loop;
  END; {consumer}
```

This approach has the advantage that there are no semaphore-type entities, nor anything resembling the set and testing of variables. Instead the conditions for entry to critical regions are explicitly given. The disadvantage of the construct is that the operations on the shared data or resource are dispersed throughout the program. It is also evident that resources and regions are going to be difficult to implement. Andrews and Schneider [1983] make the following assessment:

> Because conditions in CCR statements can contain references to local variables, each process must evaluate its own conditions. On a multi-programmed processor, this evaluation results in numerous switches of process states, many of which may be unproductive because the activated process may still find the condition false. If each process is executed on its own processor and memory is shared, however, CCR statements can be implemented quite cheaply using busy-waiting.

Conditional critical regions have been chiefly promoted by Brinch Hansen, who used them in his Edison language [Brinch Hansen, 1981], which was specially designed for multiprocessing and in 'Distributed processes' [Brinch Hansen, 1978], a notation designed for just that.

Monitors

Monitors have proved one of the more popular concurrency constructs and have been implemented in numerous languages (Concurrent Pascal [Brinch Hansen, 1975], Modula [Wirth, 1977b], Mesa [Mitchell *et al.*, 1979], Pascal-Plus [Welsh and Bustard, 1979] and Concurrent Euclid [Holt, 1982]). The idea follows on from conditional critical regions. Shared data is identified but instead of the operations being dispersed in the processes, they are named (i.e. made into procedures) and gathered together along with the data in what is essentially an abstract data type again. Variables of this type can be declared, so that one can have several resources of the same kind. For any one declared instance of the resource, the monitor guarantees that only one of its procedures will be accessing the data at any one time. Thus mutual exclusion is implicit. The little example we have been using would be rephrased thus:

```
MONITOR TYPE buffercontroller;
  DEFINITION
    buffer : string := '';
  EXCLUSIVE OPERATIONS
    deposit (string);
    fetch (string);
  IMPLEMENTATION
    -- later
END buffercontroller;
VAR B : buffercontroller;
PROCESS producer;
  VAR s : string;
  BEGIN
    loop
      create values in s;
      B.deposit (s);
    end loop;
  END; {producer}
PROCESS consumer;
  VAR s : string;
  BEGIN
    loop
      B.fetch (s);
      use the values in s;
    end loop;
  END; {consumer}
```

Conditional synchronization is, however, not hidden by the monitor construct and is achieved by semaphore-like operations. (Each language has its own slight variations.) Hoare's original proposal declares the synchronization semaphores as *conditions* and defines two operations, *wait* and *signal*, on them as follows:

- *wait* – suspends the process which called the monitor operation and relinquishes its exclusive control;
- *signal* – also suspends the process which called the monitor, and causes one of the processes waiting on this condition (if any) to be activated.

There is a difference between the type of suspension caused by the two operations. A process that suspends itself with a signal will be reactivated before any new process that is trying to get into the monitor. The implication of these operations is that, contrary to the way in which we described the mutual exclusivity of the monitor operations, there may actually be several processes in a monitor simultaneously but all but one of them will be blocked at a wait or signal.

We can now complete the monitor definition for the example:

```
IMPLEMENTATION
  full, empty : condition;
  PROCEDURE deposit (s : string);
    BEGIN
      if length(buffer) > 0 then empty.wait;
      buffer := s;
      full.signal;
    END; {deposit}
  PROCEDURE fetch (var s : string);
    BEGIN
      if length(buffer) = 0 then full.wait;
      s := buffer;
      buffer := '';
      empty.signal;
    END; {fetch}
```

As an abstraction mechanism, monitors fit nicely into the usual module or package mould, but the synchronization is crude and suffers from virtually the same problems as semaphores. Another problem is that one would tend to include instructions in monitor operations which round them off nicely from the point of view of the abstraction, but which are not concerned with the shared data and therefore should not be included in the mutual exclusivity which calling such an operation entails.

At this point it is interesting to note the approach taken by Wirth in the design of Modula-2 [Wirth, 1983]. Although clearly intended for concurrent programming, Modula-2 has no concurrent constructs as such. Instead, coroutines are provided as a basic mechanism and Wirth suggests a library module called Processes which offers routines such as Startprocess, Send, etc., which can be called to provide quasi-concurrency. With these routines, the programmer can set up monitors and, in fact, model many of the other constructs described here. Sewry [1984] has done an extensive investigation into the power of this method and was able to implement monitors and even something resembling the rendezvous, albeit with restrictions. The underlying synchronization and scheduling was not satisfactory, but could be improved by re-doing the library module. Modula-2's approach seems to fit in well with the idea of data abstraction.

Message passing

In 1978 Hoare [1978] once again presented a leap forward in concurrency with his paper entitled 'Communicating sequential processes'. (cf. Dijkstra's 'Cooperating sequential processes' ten years earlier.) The focus of this approach is the information that processes need to exchange in the normal course of their cooperation. This exchange is done by sending and receiving messages. It moves away from the shared data area approach in that a message occupies its own (hidden) storage until it is received into the storage of the receiver. At the same time, effective synchronization is achieved by procedures necessarily having to wait for messages before they can proceed.

The two operations defined for message passing are:

```
SEND values TO destination
RECEIVE variables FROM source
```

and our little example could be expressed as:

```
PROCESS producer;
  VAR s : string;
  BEGIN
    loop
      create values in s;
      SEND s TO consumer;
    end loop;
  END; {producer}
PROCESS consumer;
  VAR t : string;
    BEGIN
      loop
        RECEIVE t FROM producer;
        do something with t;
      end loop;
    END; {consumer}
```

There are two important considerations in this method. Firstly, how are the processes named, i.e. directly (as above) or in some indirect way? This point is taken up below, under Language design issues. Secondly, how do the sends and receives match up? The answer really depends on how the intermediate storage for messages is organized. If no such storage is provided, the sending process will block itself, until a corresponding receive occurs. At the other extreme, infinite storage is assumed and the sender can proceed at a rate totally independent of the receiver. In the middle is the assumption that a certain finite amount of buffer storage is available, so that the sender can get ahead of the receiver, but not by very much. The important consideration in choosing one of these approaches is that conditional synchronization, as we originally defined it, depends on the state of data produced by one process as seen by another process. If the sender gets arbitrarily ahead of the receiver, a received message may be out of date or, at the least, does not say anything about the state of the sender now.

The question of blocking applies to the receive statement too. Most commonly, it is a blocking statement, with the process waiting until a message arrives, but variations are possible. The wait may have a finite time to it, or there may be a way of testing whether a message is there before it is actually received. Using this, a process could loop around, receiving all available messages into its own storage and then attend to them as it sees fit. Another possibility is to use *guarded commands* [Dijkstra, 1975] where each message passing statement is prefaced by a condition and those that are true are eligible for execution, the choice being made non-deterministically. Andrews [1981], in his SR language, uses this facility in conjunction with remote procedure calls (discussed next).

Languages that use message passing are Gypsy [Ambler *et al.*, 1977], with buffered messages, CHILL with synchronous and buffered messages [CCITT, 1984], PLITS [Feldman, 1979] with asynchronous messages, and the CSP notation [Hoare, 1978] which has synchronous messages. CSP has been successfully implemented in the Occam language [May, 1983]. All of these are suitable for distributed processing and PLITS was specifically designed for use with a network.

Remote procedure calls

The synchronous send and receive as in message passing is a very common operation in concurrent systems and is exactly analogous to parameter passing during a procedure call. One can therefore blend both operations into a call from one process to another, known as a remote procedure. The remote procedure would either be instantiated at each call on it, with the instances executing concurrently, or it could contain a loop and service calls sequentially.

Because the first process is delayed until the second has completed its task, this kind of interaction is known as the *client–server* model, rather than the producer–consumer model used up to now. Normally, the client would provide some data to the server and expect some results back. Nevertheless, for the sake of comparison, we give the producer–consumer example again, using this construct.

```
PROCESS producer;
  VAR s : string;
  BEGIN
    loop
      create a value in s;
      CALL consumer (s);
    end loop;
  END; {producer}
PROCESS consumer (t : string);
  {instantiated at each call}
  BEGIN
    do something with t;
  END; {consumer}
```

We can now see how far we have progressed from the earlier concurrent forms. Here, the consumer has no other visible operations apart from that directly concerned with its function. All synchronizing and shared data problems have disappeared, yet the solution is just as general as those that went before. The producer may proceed at any speed without being blocked. At the same time, the consumer processes will be active only while there is work to do.

6.3 The rendezvous

The culmination of all the above features is the rendezvous, which has gained in popularity through its inclusion in Ada. Here the remote call mechanism is used, but the called part is not a procedure as such, but a sequence of statements within a procedure, introduced by an ACCEPT statement. The accept is very like a procedure header, having a name and a parameter list, e.g.

```
ACCEPT op (parameters) do ...
```

The caller must wait until the called process reaches the particular accept statement that it named, hence the term rendezvous to describe this construct. The called process executes its statements while the caller waits. At the end of the accept, they go their separate ways.

Although at first this seems like a step away from abstraction and modularity, it is not. The idea is that services, as provided in remote procedures, should once again be grouped according to their functions and the data they access. Then the accept statements are similar to the operations provided in a monitor, except that they are more versatile and powerful. We shall first give the rendezvous version of the producer–consumer example, and then describe the full features of the construct. The syntax used is not Ada's, but something simpler, since we do not believe that Ada will be the only language to have the rendezvous. The form follows that used for the description of the constructs so far.

```
PROCESS buffercontroller;
  VAR b : string;
  BEGIN
    loop
      ACCEPT deposit(a : string) do
        b := a;
      ACCEPT fetch(var a:string) do
        a := b;
    end loop;
  END; {buffercontroller}
PROCESS producer
  var s : string;
  BEGIN
    create a value in s;
    buffercontroller.deposit(s);
  END; {producer}
PROCESS consumer;
  var t : string;
  BEGIN
    buffercontroller.fetch(t);
    do something with t;
  END; {consumer}
```

The synchronization of operations is achieved by the ordering of the accept statements: a deposit must occur before a fetch. If a second deposit is initiated before the fetch is completed, the caller (i.e. producer) will be blocked until buffercontroller gets around the loop to accepting this request. Thus the rendezvous can be seen to combine the best aspects of both monitors and message passing.

There are several ways in which the basic accept statement can be used to provide very powerful facilities. These are:

1. *Order*. As we have seen, the sequential ordering of accept allows one to control the synchronization of activities.
2. *Multiple rendezvous*. By nesting accept statements, one can set up a rendezvous among several processes. For example, suppose we have two producers that provide different parts of the message that must be

sent to the consumer. Both will be making calls on deposit, and these will be accepted in either order. Buffercontroller could be phrased thus:

```
PROCESS buffercontroller;
  var b : string;
  BEGIN
    loop
      ACCEPT deposit (a1 : string) do
        ACCEPT deposit (a2 : string) do
          b := a1 & a2;
        ACCEPT fetch (var a : string) do
          a := b;
    end loop;
  END; {buffercontroller}
```

3. *Different kinds of service*. By having more than one accept with the same name, a process can service requests in different ways. For example, one could have an accept for the first request, followed by a separate one for following requests. Suppose, in our example, the consumer should receive a header message before processing those from the producer. Buffercontroller could be written as follows:

```
PROCESS buffercontroller;
  VAR b : string;
  BEGIN
    ACCEPT fetch (var a : string) do
      a := 'Listing for today' & date; {& concatenates}
    loop
      ACCEPT deposit (a : string) do
        b := a;
      ACCEPT fetch (var a : string) do
        a := b;
    end loop;
  END; {buffercontroller}
```

A process does not have to consist only of statements within accepts, and therefore executed during a rendezvous. In fact, one would endeavour to keep these statements to the minimum, and have any other non-critical work done outside the accepts. For example, the critical part of the deposit operation is the copying of the parameter into the local variable, *b*. If the string needs to be processed in some way before being sent off to the consumer, such processing can be done after the rendezvous with the producer and before a rendezvous with the consumer is initiated. The loop of buffercontroller becomes:

```
loop
  ACCEPT deposit (a : string) do
    b := a;
```

```
    trim(b); {of leading blanks}
    ACCEPT fetch (var a : string) do
      a := b;
  end loop;
```

Selecting a rendezvous

With the basic call and accept mechanism, both parties are committed once these statements are executed. For a service process, this would be too inflexible, since it would not be able to attend to someone else, if the expected call does not arrive. A rendezvous mechanism should therefore provide a SELECT statement, which in its simplest form simply allows a process to select any of the calls which are waiting, the choice being made at random. The form of the basic select statement is

```
SELECT
  ACCEPT...
OR
  ACCEPT...
OR
  .
  .
  .
END SELECT;
```

This enables a process to provide the appropriate service, depending on what comes in. For example, suppose we have two producers, one of which produces numbers that need to be converted to strings before being passed on. We could say

```
PROCESS buffercontroller;
  VAR b : string;
  BEGIN
    loop
      SELECT
        ACCEPT deposit (a : string) do
          b := a;
      OR
        ACCEPT depositnumber (n : integer) do
          b := image(n);
      END SELECT;
      ACCEPT fetch (var a : string) do
        a := b;
    end loop;
  END; {buffercontroller}
```

Here one or other of the deposits will be selected, followed by a fetch, as before.

The selection can be controlled somewhat by adding conditions to the accept statements. These operate in the same way as Dijkstra's guarded commands, as described above under message passing. At the start of a select, all the conditions are evaluated and those that are true have their accepts marked as open, together with all unconditional accepts. The subset of open accepts for which requests are pending is calculated, and one of these is chosen to proceed, the choice being made at random. Let us call these two sets *open* and *pending* respectively.

As an example, suppose we have an additional consumer that will accept only upper-case messages. Buffercontroller could be altered as follows:

```
PROCESS buffercontroller;
  VAR b : string;
  BEGIN
    loop
      ACCEPT deposit (a : string) do
        b := a;
      SELECT
        when upperonly (b) do
          ACCEPT fetchupperonly (var a : string) do
            a := b;
      OR
        ACCEPT fetch (var a : string) do
            a := b;
      END SELECT;
    end loop;
END; {buffercontroller}
```

If the message contains lowercase, the open set will consist only of the second accept and buffercontroller will wait until the original fetch is requested. Otherwise, both accepts will be open and, if both are pending as well, the message could go either way.

It is a requirement that the open set must not be empty, and the programmer has to ensure that this does not happen (by, say, including at least one accept without a condition).

Cancelling a rendezvous

If at a SELECT statement the pending set is empty, i.e. there are no requests waiting for any of the open accepts, the process waits until one does occur. This may not be desirable, and it may induce a pretty long wait because the conditions are not re-evaluated once the select has been entered. To enable a process to change its mind, an ELSE part is provided. If there are no requests, the rendezvous is cancelled, and the process continues on its own, executing the else part and then whatever follows it.

Normally the else part would either do nothing, merely serving to break the rendezvous, or would make some change to local data so that the conditions of selection are different on the next time round. To extend our example, if a mixed case message is not immediately fetched by the consumer, we could convert it to uppercase and try again, thus doubling our chances. The select above becomes:

```
SELECT
  when upperonly (b) do
    ACCEPT fetchupperonly (var a : string) do
      a := b;
OR
  ACCEPT fetch (var a : string) do
      a := b;
ELSE
  if not upperonly (b) then converttoupper(b);
END SELECT;
```

It is also possible to cancel a rendezvous from the other side by using a selected call with an else part. This kind of statement would be used by a very impatient process as it cancels the rendezvous if the service is not immediately available.

Delays

Sometimes a process does not want to cancel a rendezvous immediately, but may be prepared to wait a short while. For this reason, select statements are provided with DELAY clauses of some form or other. The effect is that, if no rendezvous takes place within the period specified by the delay, the process unblocks itself and continues on its own. The delay can also be used to provide rests between activities, which would be useful when dealing with real, but fairly slow, devices.

Terminating

Finally, the rendezvous construct must provide processes with some way of terminating. A process normally terminates when it reaches the end of its code. However, some processes, especially the server kind, are written as endless loops and need an explicit TERMINATE statement. In our example, the producer could send a "STOP" message after the last string of data, and this could be detected by buffercontroller and listed as an option in a select. This gives:

```
PROCESS buffercontroller;
  var b : string;
  BEGIN
    loop
    ACCEPT deposit (a : string) do
      b := a;
   SELECT
      when b /= "STOP" do
        ACCEPT fetch (var a : string) do
          a := b;
    OR
      when b="STOP" do
        terminate;
    END SELECT;
  end loop;
END; {buffercontroller}
```

Notice that we had to provide a condition for the fetch as well, so that it is not chosen by the non-determinism in the last case.

Processes should be provided with a means of terminating, since an enclosing (or parent) task cannot terminate until all its offspring have done so. Specific languages will have specific rules about when and where terminate can be used.

This concludes the section on the rendezvous. We have deliberately kept away from the specific syntax of Ada, since the concept is generally applicable and should be understood independently. Section 6.5 below gives a case study of Ada tasking, and an example program.

6.4 Language design issues

Given the general concurrency constructs as described in the previous two sections, we can now identify several issues for the language designer. These centre on how to relate the processes and their operations to the type and naming structure of the language.

Terminology

It is unfortunate that every language has its own terminology for the concurrency concepts, and these are often mixed up with the sequential concepts of the procedure, module and class. For grouping of data and operations, the most frequently used terms are *monitor* and *process* with exceptions being *task* (in Ada), *envelope* (in Pascal-Plus) and *region* (CHILL). For the operations themselves, procedure is most common, although Ada deviates again and uses *entry*.

The name of a process

We have up to now written processes in much the same way as procedures, with fixed names. When one process needs to call another, therefore, it would need to know its name. This is not always desirable in a large system, and various ways of indirect naming can be used instead. These fall into two categories, depending on whether the operations are grouped (as in monitors and tasks) or stand alone (as in message passing and remote procedures).

With monitors and tasks, there is fairly general agreement that two additions to direct naming are required. These are:

1. *Multiple direct.* The monitor or task is seen as a type and instances of that type may be declared, each with its own direct name. These would have separate data areas and shared code. For example, if we wanted to have a single monitor called devicehandler, and two monitors for buffers, called inbuffer and outbuffer, we could say:

   Pascal-Plus:
   ```
   ENVELOPE MODULE devicehandler;
   ...
   ENVELOPE bufferhandler;
   ...
   INSTANCE inbuffer, outbuffer : bufferhandler;
   ```

   Similarly, with Ada tasks, we would have:

   Ada:
   ```
   TASK devicehandler;
   ...
   TASK TYPE bufferhandler;
   ...
   inbuffer, outbuffer : bufferhandler;
   ```

   Calls to the various operations would use dot notation, for example:

   Ada: inbuffer.deposit or devicehandler.wakeup.

2. *Multiple indirect.* Rather than give multiple instances each a name, arrays of monitors or tasks can be declared and each individual one accessed by the usual subscripting notation. For example, if several output buffers need to be handled, we could say

   Pascal-Plus: outbuffer : array [1..n] of bufferhandler;

   and call specific operations thus:

   ```
   outbuffer[k].fetch;
   ```

In the message passing languages, the terminology resembles that of data communications, rather than of programming languages. Taken together, a source and destination define a communications *channel*, and there are several ways of naming it.

1. *One-to-one.* The actual name of the source and destination must be given, as for example in CSP [Hoare, 1978]. This can prove disadvantageous when programming client–server relationships.

2. *Many-to-many*. Sends and receives are done via globally named channels called *mailboxes*. Any process can send to a mailbox, and any process can request to receive from it. The problem is in implementation, since a message must be relayed to all processes who could possibly receive it, and after one has got it the others must be notified that it is no longer there. Gypsy uses this system, as well as the following one.
3. *Many-to-one*. A special case of a mailbox is a *port*, where only one process may receive messages through it. These are more simple to implement.

These methods all reflect static channel naming, i.e. every connection that might ever be needed in a system must be specified at compile time. It is useful to augment this with dynamic channel naming by letting variables contain channel names.

Process creation

Separate from the naming issue, is how processes start up. The simplest approach is that a process starts executing when its declaration is reached. In particular, monitors will execute their initialization code at this point. Such creation is *static*, with the number, type and identity of each process being set at compile time. A language may offer *dynamic* creation in two forms. A method used with remote procedure calls is that each time a process is called, it is instantiated with the same name, separate data and shared code. Alternatively, pointers can be used to set up processes at runtime, each with an indirect name, separate data and shared code.

CHILL uses a variation of the first method whereby a START operation will create a new instance of the process, giving it a unique instance value, which can be assigned to instance variables. A process may learn its own instance value by using the THIS operation. Ada uses the second approach with access variables being assigned to specific task types, and instances of that task type being allocated at run-time by means of NEW. As pointed out by Fidge and Pascoe [1983], Ada's approach has the virtue of orthogonality and type checking, whereas in CHILL instance variables can be assigned the value of any kind of process and are thus potential sources of error. CHILL's THIS operator is deemed useful, though.

Process topology

An issue raised by Stotts [1982] is that of describing the communication and synchronization interconnections between processes. In today's concurrency abstractions, these interconnections are implicit and embedded in the module and synchronization mechanisms. Whether it is desirable or possible to specify the topology as separate from the processes themselves is a current area of research.

Regardless of how it is specified, there is also the issue of whether the topology is static or dynamic. In a static topology, the links between processes are predictable at compile-time; in a dynamic topology they are not. The topology is independent of the method chosen for process creation. For example, both CSP and Edison allow dynamic processes, but require a static topology. Most modern languages permit a dynamic topology, and how this is used is illustrated in the next section. A fascinating, though difficult, paper by Lamb and Hilfinger [1983] uses this aspect of Ada to simulate procedure variables. Ada does not have any form of call-by-name facility, but the authors show that a reasonable approximation can be made using tasks.

6.5 A generalized dynamic system

Concurrent systems are often large and complex, unlike the copy-book examples used so far in this chapter. In order to reduce complexity, we endeavour to recognize certain standard patterns or paradigms in inter-process communication. Some of the most common are

- pipeline – data is passed from process to process in a specified order;
- client–server – high level functions pass data to low-level servers and receive results back;
- resource sharing – processes compete for the use of a single resource.

These paradigms clarify the algorithms we shall need: we still need to worry about the organization of the processes, in particular their number, types and names. Any of these properties could be static or dynamic. In the most flexible system they would all be dynamic, and we now look at how to specify such dynamic systems and assess their performance.

The problem

We shall investigate a system consisting of a number of clients and servers. The clients have various functions that need to be performed and they delegate these to the servers. We wish to observe the following degrees of freedom:

- the number of servers should vary with demand,
- different types of servers may provide functionally the same service,
- servers are allocated on request, not dedicated to a client.

Put succinctly, this means that the way in which requests by a client for a given function are handled must be independent of the number, type or name of servers. The solution presented below owes much to the work of Olivier Roubine (recently published in Roubine [1985]).

Elements of a solution

We shall propose a solution in Ada, using the rendezvous to the full. The provision of the three requirements can be made using Ada's features as follows:

1. *Number*. Access types to server tasks enable us to create new servers at will.
2. *Type*. Each server task declares an interface task which is implemented as a pointer to a task of a fixed type. It is these interface tasks that are then passed around in the allocation process. Although the interfaces are all of the same type, the servers need not be.
3. *Name*. Between the client and servers we insert a dispatcher task whose job it is to keep a list of pointers to free servers and to allocate these as required. Thus the client need never know the name of a server.

Figure 6.2 gives a diagrammatic view of the system we are proposing, showing one group of servers providing functionally the same service. On it is indicated the protocol of calls that will achieve the necessary communication and synchronization between the tasks. The *active* or caller tasks are:

- *Clients*. Each client calls the dispatcher with a find and gets access to a server interface in return. It then issues a request on this server interface.
- *Servers*. When ready, each server signals the dispatcher that it is available and then issues a start to its interface. Similarly it issues a finish when its job is complete.

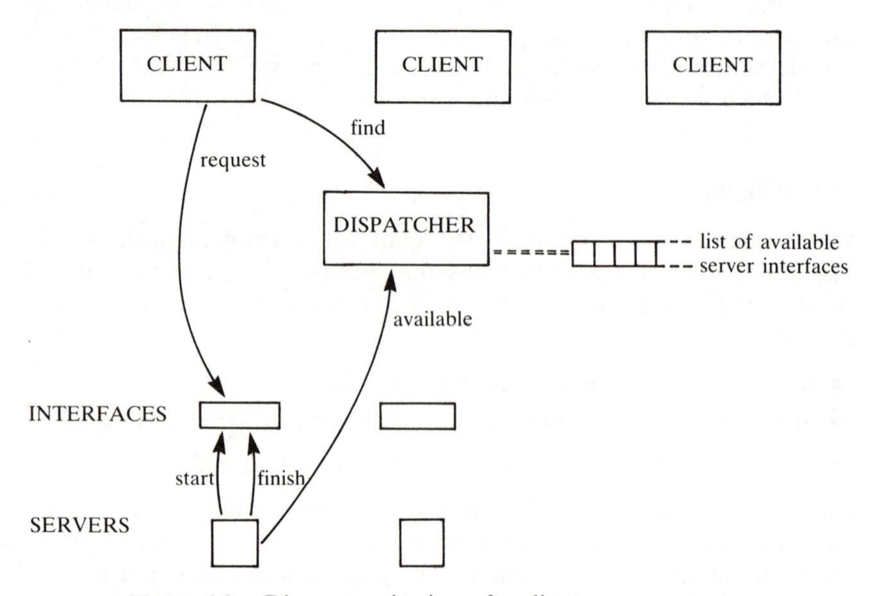

Figure 6.2 Diagrammatic view of a client–server system

The *passive* or accepting tasks are:

- *Dispatcher*. Accepts availables and finds in order to manipulate the pool of servers.
- *Interfaces*. Each accepts request and start to arrange a three-way rendezvous, transferring any data from the client to the server, and any results back again once a finish call is received.

The solution in Ada

In order to understand the system, we shall look at it bit by bit. First, the body of an interface:

```
TASK BODY interfaces IS
  BEGIN
    LOOP
      ACCEPT request (D : in data; R : out results) do
        accept start (input : out data) do
          input := D;
        end start;
        accept finish (output : in results) do
          R := output;
        end finish;
      END request;
    END LOOP;
  END interfaces;
```

Interfaces will be defined as a task type, with the pointers to it defined as

```
TYPE to_interfaces is access interfaces;
```

The dispatcher, on the other hand, is a single task whose body is:

```
TASK BODY dispatcher is
  -- declaration of the data structure for the pool
  -- of available interfaces, including
  FUNCTION empty RETURN boolean;
  -- which is true if no interfaces are available
  BEGIN
    LOOP
      SELECT
        accept available (i : in to_interfaces) do
          -- save i in the pool;
        end available;
      OR when not empty =>
        accept find (i : out to_interfaces) do
          i := -- some interface from the pool;
        end find;
      END SELECT;
    END LOOP;
  END dispatcher;
```

The servers themselves will be defined as any task type, provided that they

1. create an interface using

```
interface : to_interfaces := NEW interfaces;
```

2. observe a protocol of calls on available, start and finish in that order, i.e.

```
LOOP
  dispatcher.available (interface);
  interface.start(...); -- parameters of type data
  .
    -- perform the service
  .
  interface.finish(...); -- parameters of type results
END LOOP;
```

Finally, we have the client which, like the servers, can be any task provided it

1. declares a holder for the name of the server interface that it will be allocated, i.e.

```
s : to_interfaces;
```

2. issues calls in pairs as follows:

```
dispatcher.find(s);
s.request(...,...); -- data and results parameters
```

The tasks required by the system itself are the client and the servers. The dispatcher and the interfaces are necessitated by the solution but they are generally applicable to any function required in a client–server environment, the only variation being the type of data passed back and forth. We can therefore express these tasks as part of a generic package, which can be instantiated for each functionally different request.

The generic declaration, together with the specification parts of these two tasks, is:

```
GENERIC
  TYPE data is private;
  TYPE results is private;
PACKAGE interface_handler is
  TASK TYPE interfaces is
    ENTRY request (D : IN data; R : OUT results);
    ENTRY start    (input : OUT data);
    ENTRY finish   (output : IN results);
  END interfaces;
  TYPE to_interfaces is ACCESS interfaces;
  TASK dispatcher is
    ENTRY available (i : IN to_interfaces);
    ENTRY find      (i : OUT to_interfaces);
  END dispatcher;
END interface_handler;
```

The full program to test this method with two kinds of servers – the readers and writers – and a client that simply wants a message read and written, is given in Figure 6.3, with portions of the output in Figure 6.4. The output gives short annotations about what is happening, under columns for each task kind. The numbers refer to numbers allocated to each of the dynamic tasks by the create procedure in the printer package. The final report from the Ada system at the end shows the status of all the infinite tasks (those with no terminate option) once the finite client tasks have ended. If followed through by hand, this kind of output enables one to become aware of the interaction of the tasks, and more familiar with concurrent processing.

Scheduling requests

In the system as it stands, clients have to queue at the dispatcher if no server is immediately available. This queue is caused by the conditional accept

```
when not empty =>
  ACCEPT find (i : out to_interfaces);
    i := -- some interface from the pool;
  END find;
```

If the servers are very busy and the queue builds up, it may not be appropriate simply to select the next client in line; clients could well have different demands and constraints which would give them different priorities. Ada provides a facility whereby an entry can be replaced by a *family of entries* thus giving multiple queues at a single point. This is specified as follows:

```
TYPE priorities is integer range 1..16;
ENTRY find (priorities) (i : out to_interfaces);
```

and each client would call find with its own priority, e.g.

```
dispatcher.find(4)(s);
```

Once a server is available, the dispatcher must be able to select the waiting client with the highest priority. It can do this in two ways – by polling or by signing in. Polling is done thus:

```
FOR p in priorities loop
  SELECT
    ACCEPT find (p) (i : out to_interfaces) do
      i := -- some interface from the pool;
    END find;
    exit; -- the loop
  ELSE
    null;
  END select;
END LOOP;
```

```
WITH text_io; USE text_io;
PROCEDURE test_tasking IS
-- A program to illustrate dynamic allocation of
-- server tasks (the readers and writers) to clients
-- using interfaces and dispatchers. Ada features used
-- include accesses to task types and generic tasks.
--                                  J.M. Bishop

--------------------------------------------------------------------
------------------ BASIC DECLARATIONS ----------------------------

TASK TYPE readers;
TYPE to_readers is access readers;
TASK TYPE writers;
TYPE to_writers is access writers;
TASK TYPE clients;
TYPE to_clients is access clients;
SUBTYPE messages is string(1..25);
SUBTYPE irrelevant is integer; -- readers do not need input
zero : irrelevant := 0;        -- and writers do not need output

---------------------------------------------------------------------
------------------- PRINTER PACKAGE --------------------------------

  PACKAGE printer IS
  -- A package to enable the names of tasks to be
  -- written out, and the actions they take to be
  -- recorded under columns for each task kind.
    TYPE     kinds    is (client,dispatch,interface,reader,writer);
    SUBTYPE columns is integer range 1..80;
    SUBTYPE names    is integer RANGE  0..4;
    column   : array(kinds) of columns := (1,15,30,45,60);
    spaces   : CONSTANT string(columns)
             := (columns'first..columns'last => ' ');
    PROCEDURE create(kind:in kinds; name:out names; n:out string);
  END printer;

  PACKAGE BODY printer is
    count : array(kinds) of names := (kinds'first..kinds'last=>0);
    PROCEDURE create (kind:in kinds; name:out names; n:out string) is
    BEGIN
      count(kind) := count(kind) + 1;
      name := count(kind);
      n := spaces(1..column(kind)) & names'image(name);
      put_line (n & " created");
    END create;
  END printer;
  USE printer;

-------------------------------------------------------------------
------------------- INTERFACE_HANDLER PACKAGE -------------------

  GENERIC
  -- A package containing the task Dispatcher
  -- and task type Interface which are
  -- instantiated for each kind of server.
    kind : IN kinds;
    TYPE data IS private;
    TYPE results IS private;

  PACKAGE interface_handler IS
    PROCEDURE service (D : IN data; R : OUT results);
    TASK TYPE interfaces IS
      ENTRY request (D : IN data; R : OUT results);
      ENTRY start    (input : OUT data);
      ENTRY finish   (output : IN results);
    END interfaces;

    TYPE to_interfaces IS ACCESS interfaces;
```

(continued)

```
    TASK dispatcher IS
      ENTRY available (i : IN to_interfaces);
      ENTRY find      (i : OUT to_interfaces);
    END dispatcher;
  END interface_handler;

  PACKAGE BODY interface_handler IS
    TASK BODY interfaces IS
      name   : names;
      n      : string(1..column(interface)+names'width);
    BEGIN
      create(interface,name,n);
      LOOP
        ACCEPT request (D : IN data; R : OUT results) DO
          put_line(n & " requested");
          accept start (input : OUT data) do
            put_line(n & " started");
            input := D;
          end start;
          accept finish (output : in results) do
            put_line(n & " finished");
            R := output;
          end finish;
        END request;
      END LOOP;
    END interfaces;

    PROCEDURE service(D : in data; R : out results) IS
      s : to_interfaces;
      c : string(1..column(client)) := spaces(1..column(client));
      k : string(1..6) := kinds'image(kind);
    BEGIN
      put_line (c & " Find " & k);
      dispatcher.find(s);
      put_line (c & " Request " & k);
      s.request(D,R);
    END service;

    TASK BODY dispatcher is
      SUBTYPE pool_range is integer range 1..10;
      pool     : ARRAY (pool_range) OF to_interfaces;
      size     : pool_range := 1;
      n        : string(1..column(dispatch)+6)
               := spaces(1..column(dispatch))&kinds'image(kind);
    BEGIN
      put_line(n & " Dispatcher created");
      LOOP
        SELECT
          ACCEPT available (i : IN to_interfaces) DO

            put_line(n & " available");
            pool(size) := i;
            size := size + 1;
          END available;
        OR WHEN size>1 => --NOT empty
          ACCEPT find(i : OUT to_interfaces) DO
            put_line(n & " found ");
            size := size - 1;
            i := pool(size);
          END find;
        END SELECT;
      END LOOP;
    END dispatcher;
  END interface_handler;

-------------------------------------------------------------
------------------ READER_HANDLER and READERS ---------------

  PACKAGE reader_handler IS
          NEW interface_handler (kind => reader,data => irrelevant,
                                 results => messages);
```

(continued)

```
  USE reader_handler;

  TASK BODY readers IS
    name      : names;
    interface : reader_handler.to_interfaces
              := NEW reader_handler.interfaces;
    message   : messages;
    n         : string(1..column(reader)+names'width);
  BEGIN
    create(reader,name,n);
    LOOP
      put_line(n & " available");
      reader_handler.dispatcher.available (interface);
      put_line(n & " start");
      readers.interface.start(zero);
      put_line (n & " --READING--");
      get(message); skip_line;
      put_line(n & " finish");
      readers.interface.finish(message);
    END LOOP;
  END readers;

-------------------------------------------------------------------------
------------------- WRITER_HANDLER and WRITERS ----------------------

  PACKAGE writer_handler IS
        NEW interface_handler (kind => writer, data => messages,
                               results => irrelevant);
  USE writer_handler;

  TASK BODY writers IS
    name      : names;
    interface : writer_handler.to_interfaces
              := NEW writer_handler.interfaces;
    message   : messages;
    n         : string(1..column(writer)+names'width);
  BEGIN
    create(writer,name,n);
    LOOP
      put_line(n & " available");
      writer_handler.dispatcher.available (interface);
      put_line(n & " start");
      writers.interface.start(message);
      put_line(n & "--WRITING--");
      put_line (' ' & message);
      put_line(n & " finish");
      writers.interface.finish (0);
    END LOOP;
  END writers;

-------------------------------------------------------------------------
------------------- CLIENTS ---------------------------------------

  TASK BODY clients IS
    name    : names;
    message : messages;
    n       : string(1..column(client)+names'width);
  BEGIN
    create(client,name,n);
    FOR i IN 1..2 LOOP
      put_line(n & " read");
      reader_handler.service (0, message);
      put_line(n & " write");
      writer_handler.service (message, zero);
    END LOOP;
  END clients;

-------------------------------------------------------------------------
------------------- MAIN PROGRAM ----------------------------------

BEGIN
  DECLARE
```

(continued)

```
      reader : to_readers;
      writer : to_writers;
      client : to_clients;
    BEGIN
      FOR k in kinds LOOP
        set_col(3+positive_count(column(k))); put(kinds'image(k));
      END LOOP;
      new_line;
      FOR i IN 1..2 LOOP
        reader := NEW readers;
      END LOOP;
      FOR i IN 1..2 LOOP
        writer := NEW writers;
      END LOOP;
      FOR i IN 1..3 LOOP
        client := NEW clients;
      END LOOP;
    END;
  END test_tasking;
```

Figure 6.3 Ada program for a client–server system

```
             READER Dispatcher created
             WRITER Dispatcher created
 CLIENT         DISPATCH          INTERFACE       READER          WRITER
                                  1 created
                                                  1 created
                                                  1 available
             READER available
                                                  1 start
                                  2 created
                                                  2 created
                                                  2 available
             READER available
                                                  2 start
                                  3 created
                                                                  1 created
                                                                  1 available
             WRITER available
                                                                  1 start
                                  4 created
                                                                  2 created
                                                                  2 available
             WRITER available
1 created
1 read
                                                                  2 start
Find READER
             READER found
2 created
2 read
Find READER
             READER found
Request READER
                                  2 requested
                                  2 started
Request READER
                                  1 requested
                                  1 started
                                                  1 --READING--
                                                  1 finish
                                  1 finished
                                                  2 --READING--
                                                  1 available
3 created
3 read
```

(continued)

```
 Find READER
                                                    2 finish
 2 write
 Find WRITER
             WRITER found
             READER available
                              2 finished
 Request WRITER
                              4 requested
                              4 started
             READER found
                                                    1 start
                                                    2 available
                                                                  2--WRITING--
***** First message
...
... etc.
...
***** Sixth message
                                                                  2 finish
                              4 finished
                                                                  2 available
             WRITER available
                                                                  2 start
  System inactive

THE FOLLOWING TASKS ARE WAITING FOR ACCESS TO ENTRIES :
-----------------------------------------------------------------------

TASK TEST_TASKING.READERS IS QUEUED ON ENTRY START #1 OF TASK
                              TEST_TASKING.READER_HANDLER.INTERFACES
TASK TEST_TASKING.WRITERS IS QUEUED ON ENTRY START #1 OF TASK
                              TEST_TASKING.WRITER_HANDLER.INTERFACES
*    *    *    *    *    *    *    *    *    *    *    *    *    *

TASK TEST_TASKING.WRITERS IS QUEUED ON ENTRY START #1 OF TASK
                              TEST_TASKING.WRITER_HANDLER.INTERFACES
TASK TEST_TASKING.READERS IS QUEUED ON ENTRY START #1 OF TASK
                              TEST_TASKING.READER_HANDLER.INTERFACES
*    *    *    *    *    *    *    *    *    *    *    *    *    *

THE FOLLOWING TASKS ARE WAITING FOR CALL ON ENTRIES :
-----------------------------------------------------------------------

TASK TEST_TASKING.WRITER_HANDLER.INTERFACES HAS ENTRY REQUEST #1
                                        OPEN FOR RENDEZVOUS

TASK TEST_TASKING.WRITER_HANDLER.INTERFACES HAS ENTRY REQUEST #1
                                        OPEN FOR RENDEZVOUS

TASK TEST_TASKING.READER_HANDLER.DISPATCHER HAS ENTRY FIND #1
                                        OPEN FOR RENDEZVOUS
TASK TEST_TASKING.READER_HANDLER.DISPATCHER HAS ENTRY AVAILABLE #1
                                        OPEN FOR RENDEZVOUS

TASK TEST_TASKING.READER_HANDLER.INTERFACES HAS ENTRY REQUEST #1
                                        OPEN FOR RENDEZVOUS

TASK TEST_TASKING.READER_HANDLER.INTERFACES HAS ENTRY REQUEST #1
                                        OPEN FOR RENDEZVOUS

TASK TEST_TASKING.WRITER_HANDLER.DISPATCHER HAS ENTRY FIND #1
                                        OPEN FOR RENDEZVOUS
TASK TEST_TASKING.WRITER_HANDLER.DISPATCHER HAS ENTRY AVAILABLE #1
                                        OPEN FOR RENDEZVOUS
```

Figure 6.4 Output from the client–server system

A more efficient method is for the find to be done in two stages. Firstly, the client 'signs on' and gives the dispatcher its priority. The dispatcher records this number. When there are no more sign-ons from clients or availables from servers, the dispatcher looks to see if it can effect a match, i.e. a server is available and at least one client has signed on. It then chooses the highest priority number and issues a find on that particular queue. This has the effect of establishing a rendezvous with the client who first joined that queue. We can therefore choose between priorities, but, within a priority group, requests are handled in sequence. The dispatcher now becomes:

```
TASK dispatcher is
  ENTRY available (i : IN to_interface);
  ENTRY sign_on (p : in priorities);
  ENTRY find (priorities) (i : OUT to_interface);
END dispatcher;
TASK BODY dispatcher is
  -- declaration of the data structure for the pool
  -- of available interfaces, including
  FUNCTION empty RETURN boolean;
  -- which is true if no interfaces are available
  queue : array (priorities) of integer
    := (priorities'first..priorities'last => 0);
  queued : integer := 0;
  BEGIN
    LOOP
      SELECT
        accept available (i : to_interfaces) do
          -- save i in the pool;
        end available;
      OR when not empty =>
        ACCEPT sign_on (p : in priorities) do
          queue(p) := queue(p) + 1;
          queued := queued + 1;
        end sign_on;
      ELSE
        null;
      END SELECT;
      IF not empty and queued > 0 then
        FOR p in priorities loop
          IF queued(p) > 0 then
            ACCEPT find (p) (i : out to_interfaces) do
            i := -- a suitable interface from pool;
          END find;
          queue(p) := queue(p)-1;
          queued := queued - 1;
          exit; -- the loop
        END IF;
      END LOOP;
    END IF;
  END LOOP;
END dispatcher;
```

To make use of this revised dispatcher, the clients must issue three calls in succession. These can be neatly grouped in a procedure to which the client gives its priority and input parameters, receiving output parameters in return. Notice that the existence of the serve interface can therefore be transparent to the client. This procedure would be part of the interface_handler package.

```
PROCEDURE serve (p : in priorities; D : in data; R : out results) is
  s : to_interfaces;
  BEGIN
    dispatcher.sign_on(p);
    dispatcher.find (P) (s);
    s.request (D,R);
  END serve;
```

Assessment

This solution fulfils the goals set and is remarkably flexible. It is also extensible in that new types of requests can be added simply by instantiating the interface_handler package. New servers can be added at run-time by allocating them through the access types. New clients can be added at will, since no one else in the system needs to know the names of clients.

A question is whether it is efficient. The introduction of interface tasks for every server can lead to inefficiencies in that extra process switching is required. Fortunately tasks of this kind are subject to an optimization in implementation. Habermann and Nassi [1980] discovered that a task that contains only accept and select statements (possibly in loops) need not physically exist but may have its actions performed in the body of its caller. Thus the server interfaces and the original dispatcher would not reduce the efficiency of the system. However, the dispatcher programmed with a scheduling capability will be an active task in its own right.

In conclusion, it seems that abstraction techniques can be applied very effectively in concurrent systems, given a reasonable set of constructs. By carefully designing the algorithms and process organizations so that they maximize modularity and keep interaction to a minimum, efficient tasking systems will result.

Other systems

The other paradigms for concurrent systems mentioned above cannot be covered in a book of this nature, and the reader is referred to the work of Gehani [1983] for examples in Ada and Hoare [1974, 1978] for examples using monitors and CSP.

Exercises

1. Discuss the evolution of language features for concurrent programming, from semaphores through critical regions to monitors. Illustrate your discussion with examples from languages such as Modula-2 and Ada.
2. Discuss the concurrent facilities provided by Ada, illustrating your answer with Roubine's classic transaction system. Show how the internal Habermann–Nassi optimization can be applied to minimize the number of actual tasks at run-time.
3. Compare the status of tasks and procedures in Ada, paying special attention to the ways in which procedure variables can be implemented.
4. Describe and differentiate between the 'message' and 'transaction' approaches used by Roubine [1985] to implement a client–server system. Give an outline of the Ada implementation of both approaches, noting any difficulties or optimizations resulting from features of the language.
5. A classic technique for obtaining flexibility and extensibility is to apply indirection. Show how indirection can be used in both data and actions to achieve these goals in a general client–server system. Illustrate your answer with diagrams or Ada code as appropriate.

References

Ambler, A.L., Good, D.I., Browne, J.C., Burger, W.F., Cohen, R.M., Hoch, C.G. and Wells, R.E., 1977. 'GYPSY – a language for specification and implementation of verifiable programs', Proceedings of LDRS. In *SIGPLAN*, **12(3)**, 1–10.

Andrews, G.R., 1981. 'Synchronising resources', *TOPLAS*, **3(4)**, 405–430.

Andrews, G.R. and Schneider, F.B., 1983. 'Concepts and notations for concurrent programming', *Computing Surveys*, **15(1)**, 3–44.

Brinch Hansen, P., 1973. *Operating System Principles*, New Jersey, Prentice-Hall.

Brinch Hansen, P., 1975. 'The programming language Concurrent Pascal', *IEEE-SE*, 1(2), 199–206.

Brinch Hansen, P., 1978. 'Distributed processes – a concurrent programming concept', *CACM*, **21(11)**, 934–941.

Brinch Hansen, P., 1981. 'The Edison papers', *SPE*, **11(4)**, 323–414.

CCITT Study Group XI, 1984. *CHILL User's Manual*, CHILL Bulletin, **4(1)**.

Dijkstra, E.W., 1968. 'Cooperating sequential processes'. In *Programming Languages*, edited by F. Genuys, New York, Academic Press, pp. 43–112.

Dijkstra, E.W., 1975. 'Guarded commands, nondeterminism and formal derivation of programs', *CACM*, **18(8)**, 453–457.

Feldman, J.A., 1979. 'High level programming for distributed computing', *CACM*, **22(6)**, 353–368.

Fidge, C.J. and Pascoe, R.S.V., 1983. 'A comparison of the concurrency concepts and module facilities of CHILL and Ada', *Australian Computer Journal*, **15(1)**, 17–27.

Gehani, N., 1983. *Ada – An Advanced Introduction*, New Jersey, Prentice-Hall.

Habermann, A.N. and Nassi, I., 1980. *Efficient Implementation of Ada Tasks*, Carnegie-Mellon University, Pittsburg USA, Technical Report CMU-CS-80-103.

Hoare, C.A.R., 1972. 'Towards a theory of parallel programming'. In *Operating Systems Techniques*, edited by C.A.R. Hoare and R.H. Perrott, New York, Academic Press, pp. 61–71.

Hoare, C.A.R., 1974. 'Monitors: an operating system structuring concept', *CACM*, **17(10)**, 549–557.

Hoare, C.A.R., 1978. 'Communicating sequential processes', *CACM*, **21(8)**, 666–677.

Holt, R.C., 1982. 'A short introduction to Concurrent Euclid', *SIGPLAN*, **17(5)**, 60–79.

Lamb, D.A. and Hilfinger, P.N., 1983. 'Simulation of procedure variables using Ada tasks', *IEEE-SE*, **9(1)**, 13–15.

May, D., 1983. 'Occam', *SIGPLAN*, **18(4)**, 69–79.

Mitchell, J.G., Maybury, W. and Sweet, R., 1979. *Mesa Language Manual Version 5.0*, Report CSL-79-3, Xerox Palo Alto Research Centre.

Roubine, O., 1985. 'Programming large and flexible systems in Ada', *Proceedings of the Ada International Conference Ada in Use*, Paris, May 1985, edited by J.G.P. Barnes and G.A. Fisher, Cambridge University Press, pp. 197–209 (also printed as *Ada Letters*, **V**, 2, 1985).

Sewry, D.A., 1984. *Concurrency in Modula-2*, M.Sc. thesis, Rhodes University, Grahamstown RSA (printed partially, 1984, in *SIGPLAN*, **19(11)**, 23–41).

Stotts, P.D., 1982. 'A comparative study of concurrent programming languages', *SIGPLAN*, **17(10)**, 50–61.

Welsh, J. and Bustard, D.W., 1979. 'Pascal-Plus – another language for modular programming', *SPE*, **9(11)**, 947–957.

Welsh, J. and Lister, A., 1981. 'A comparative study of task communication in Ada', *SPE*, **11(3)**, 257–290.

Wirth, N., 1977a. 'Towards a discipline of real-time programming', *CACM*, **20(8)**, 577–583.

Wirth, N., 1977b. 'The Modula Papers', *SPE*, **7(1)**, 3–84.

Wirth, N., 1983. *Programming in Modula-2*, 2nd edn., Berlin, Springer-Verlag.

Wortmann, D.B., 1977. 'Introduction to LDRS', *SIGPLAN*, **12(3)**, iii.

Chapter 7 Data Protection and Access Control

The data abstraction issues discussed so far have centred on the design and incorporation of data types into a language and their use in writing relatively self-contained modules. The real world extends beyond these boundaries and we now consider how data abstraction functions when objects must be shared between modules. The issues involved are protection and control of access at different levels, the implementation of this control and the handling of exceptions.

7.1 The origins of protection

> Protection in a programming language is the ability to express directly the desired access control relationships for all objects in a language.
>
> [Ambler and Hoch, 1977]

Data protection and access control began seriously with the definition of Algol 60 and the concept of scope. Scope enables the identifier for an object to be known in the block in which it is first declared and in all the enclosed blocks in which it is not redeclared. Ever since then, the term *block-structured language* has been synonymous with high level language and block structuring is an enduring basis for language design.

In a block-structured language, the ability to access data is decided at compile-time; that is, the protection is static. If identifiers are within the required scope then the objects they name are accessible, otherwise not. The compiler checks the use of identifiers by means of a remarkably simple naming mechanism. Each identifier in a block is given a name consisting of (level, number), where level is a measure of the nesting of the block and number is a serial number for identifiers within the block. Figure 7.1 shows an example of such naming, with the arrows indicating what is visible from where.

The rule of scope put formally, then, states that at any block n the identifiers at the enclosing levels from level $n-1$ outwards are accessible. There is no conflict between the identifiers in the blocks B and C in the example, since they are mutually exclusive. When checking access from block D, only C and A are enclosing and therefore visible. Scope is affected if a visible identifier is redeclared. This is known as *occlusion* and the new identifier hides the old one, rendering the name of the outer object invisible.

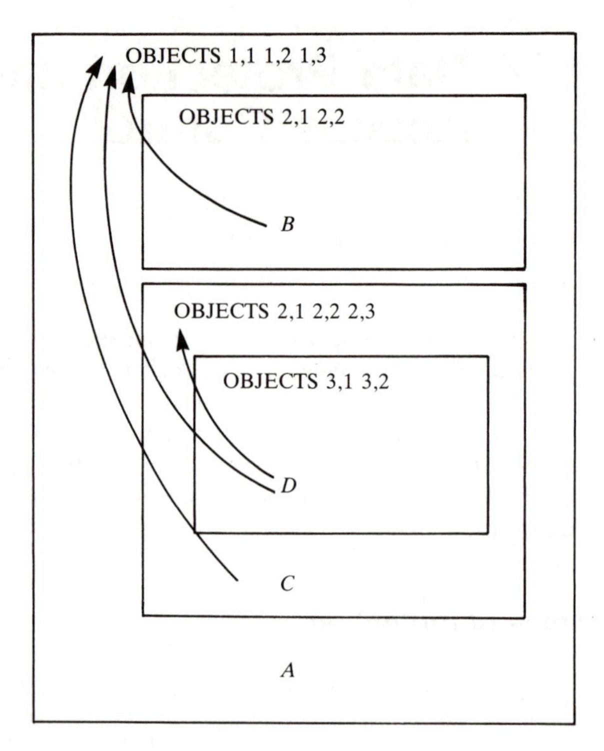

Figure 7.1 Access control using simple scope

Scope at run-time

Although not at issue here, it is interesting to note that the run-time representation of block structure is traditionally a stack, with the data for each block forming a frame and access to currently 'live' frames being governed by a display or set of linked lists [Bishop and Barron, 1980]. The sequence of calls to blocks is quite independent of the static decisions on protection, but these decisions are still mirrored in the display and lexical chains maintained at run-time. Suppose the sequence of calls in the above example was

A C B A C D

then we would have a stack and display as shown in Figure 7.2. The lexical chains link frames at the same level so that as a block is exited the previous one becomes active through the display.

Not everyone has used the stack model for illustration and during the seventies there was a strong push for using a contour model which helped to show the block structure (and hence the protection) alongside the current state of execution [Johnston, 1971; Organick, 1973]. Although the simple

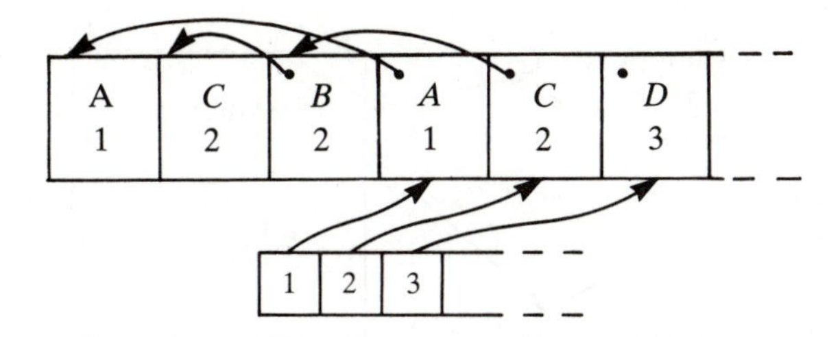

Figure 7.2 Stack and display for the call sequence *ACBACD*

stack model has stood the test of time, the ideas of the contour model have aided the depiction of later more complex protection mechanisms based on dynamic decisions.

Before looking in detail at how the access control of block-structured languages can be used in practice, we briefly note the methods used in the early non-block-structured languages.

Access control in early languages

The control of access to data in the still widely used languages, BASIC and COBOL, is governed by the fact that each has a single data area. Thus, in simple form, all data is accessible everywhere. The picture would be as in Figure 7.3 with the arrows indicating visibility as before.

Of the same vintage, but now starting to wane in popularity, FORTRAN had a more sophisticated system. Objects could be local to a routine and inaccessible elsewhere. To make them accessible, the usual parameter passing facility was available or else one could use COMMON

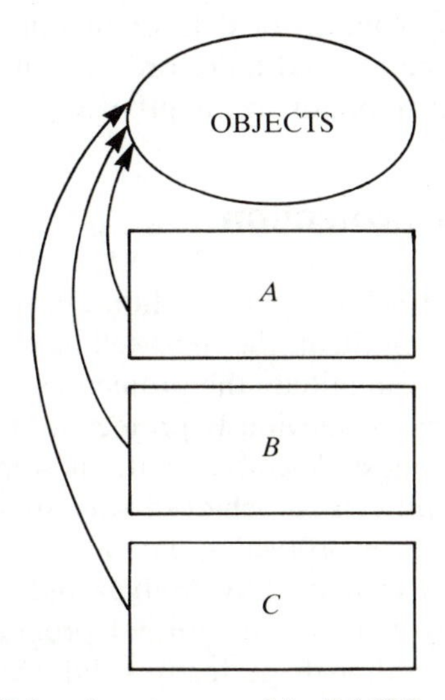

Figure 7.3 Access control in BASIC and COBOL

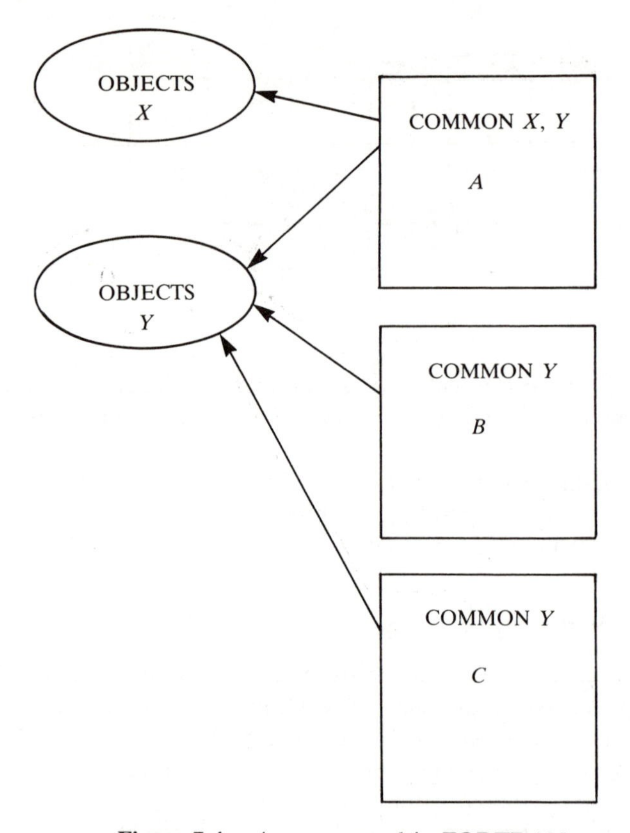

Figure 7.4 Access control in FORTRAN

blocks, as described in Section 1.2. This was an early explicit access control mechanism. There was no concept of data originating or belonging to one routine – the data was separate and therefore shareable by all who wanted it. Figure 7.4 shows an example of this approach.

7.2 Procedural level protection

There are several ways of achieving protection and control of data at the procedural level. In assessing them, the most telling criterion is whether the routine that owns the data can initiate the protection or whether it must rely on the cooperation of its users. Obviously protection which can be governed entirely by the owner is most desirable, but, in some of the techniques described below, quite a bit can be achieved with some cooperation.

The methods that exist for protecting data at the procedural level were highlighted and thoroughly examined by Ambler and Hoch [1977]. Some of the methods they identify fall in with normal programming practice and some seem very strange, although perfectly valid. At this level, the four methods are:

- named types.
- parameter mechanisms,
- scope and nesting,
- routines as parameters.

Named types

This was one of Pascal's great advances (although Algol 68 had a similar concept earlier). Instead of relying on a type being correctly and identically described wherever it is needed, Pascal provided for a type to be described once and given a name. Thereafter, wherever the name is used, the properties of the type are available. At the time the language was defined, it was not appreciated what a powerful protection tool this was, and those using the language and writing translators for it had differing views as to whether the naming was essential for type equality. The idea of structural equivalence – two objects being the same if they have the same structure, never mind their type names – was shot down by Welsh *et al.* [1977]. The ANSI/BSI Pascal Standard which was finalized in 1982 uses only name equivalence, and so does Ada. It is interesting to note, however, that structural equivalence is still alive and well in CHILL, as promoted in a comparative study with Ada [Boute and Jackson, 1981], and in Algol 68.

What we achieve with named types is protection against accidental misuse of data and the protection is entirely initiated by the owner.

Parameter mechanisms

The pass-by-value parameter mechanism provides protection from altering actual values passed to a procedure. In Pascal-like languages, the owner institutes protection of the user's data. It is interesting to remember that in PL/1 the user routine had to institute the protection itself as the parameter passing mechanism depended on whether a variable or an expression was being passed. Variables were passed by reference and expressions by value. In order to pass a variable by value it had to be 'converted' into an expression by putting it in parenthesis.

Scope and nesting

By declaring data locally, a procedure can initiate its own protection. The difficulty comes when several procedures at the same level (i.e. unnested) want to share data and yet protect it from other procedures. The only way to share data under ordinary scope rules is to declare it all globally (which will not give any protection) or to pass everything as parameters (which may be prohibitively expensive). This requirement led to modules and packages, which are discussed in the next section.

Order of definition can also give protection; for instance, if variables can

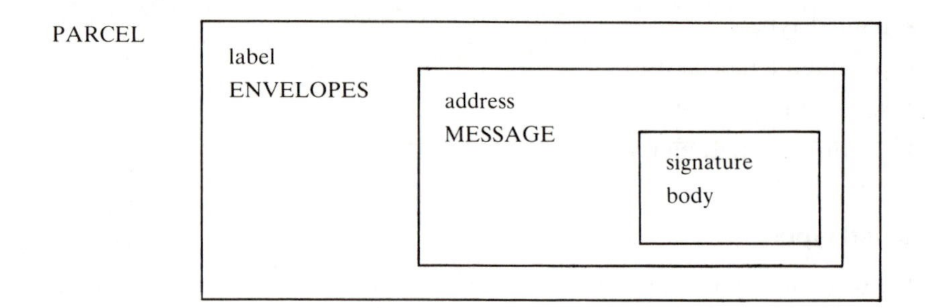

Figure 7.5 Prison Mail System

be declared after procedures, they are protected from use by those procedures. Few of the older languages permit this, and it does rely entirely on everyone agreeing to the order.

Once data is defined in an enclosing scope, all procedures can use it – and fully. The danger of such freedom and a way around it was illustrated in Ambler and Hoch's Prison Mail System. In their example, prisoners in a prison write signed messages which are put into envelopes and addressed. Each prisoner bundles all his envelopes into a parcel and labels it, as shown in Figure 7.5. The parcels are collected by the guards and given to a postmaster who opens them, sorts the envelopes according to addresses and makes up new parcels for distribution back to the prisoners by the guards. The protection required is natural, i.e.

- the prisoners can read and write bodies, signatures, addresses and labels;
- the postmaster can read addresses and read and write labels;
- the guards can only read labels.

All three groups must handle the outer level of data (the parcels) but we need to restrict access selectively to the inner levels. The only way of doing this is to hide each type by occlusion. The postmaster and guards respectively must agree to define a dummy type for each of those that they should not see, i.e.

```
Pascal: TYPE   messages =  record
                             signature : string;
                             body      : string;
                           end;
               envelopes = record
                             address   : addresses;
                             message   : messages;
                           end;
               parcels =   record
                             label     : labels;
                             envelope  : envelopes;
                           end;
```

```
PROCEDURE guard (parcel : parcels);
  TYPE envelopes = integer;
  ...
PROCEDURE postmaster (parcel : parcels);
  TYPE messages = integer;
  ...
```

Thus the guard's procedure can assign parcels as a whole as well as label and envelope fields, but it cannot create variables of the original envelopes type and thereby copy a letter from its parcel and examine it.

As a protection mechanism, occlusion does not rate very highly. It relies on the user initiating the protection; it is unnatural; and most of all it does not stop the guard, for instance, from simply looking in the parcel by means of record field selection. We need the next method in order to protect against such ordinary use.

Routines as parameters

The solutions to the Prison Mail System problem make great use of indirect access to data. Instead of passing a parcel to the guards or postmaster, procedures to readlabels, writelabels, sortparcels, etc., are passed instead. The variables are then defined in the scope of these procedures, but not in the scope of the guards and postmaster. They get access to the data via the procedures.

This is a very secure method but very tedious to set up. Moreover, procedure parameters are definitely out of fashion, having been excluded from several post-Pascal languages including Euclid, Gypsy and Ada.

Protection keys

One further method which is popular in operating systems and is a feature of CLU is the ability to construct unique, unfabricatable protection keys. This relies on a strong definition of equality, i.e. two variables are equal only if they are the same object (the usual meaning of equal is called 'similar'). In the CLU solution to the Prison Mail problem, access to the data is via access procedures which are additionally protected by having a key as a parameter. The main program creates two such keys – corresponding to being able to access messages and envelopes respectively – and passes them to the routines as appropriate. The routines then need these keys to get the access operations to work.

There is a high level of protection here, at very little cost, but the concept has not caught on in later languages.

7.3 Module level protection

Proper data protection, initiated by the owner, did not come about until the advent of data abstraction. As soon as routines could be defined along with the data they used and encapsulated with it in a module, access to that data could be controlled. There are several levels and methods of control and rather than discuss them by language (as is done by Ambler and Hoch's study [1977]), I endeavour here to classify the methods and to use the various languages for illustration.

Control of visibility to other modules

According to normal scope rules, all objects declared by a module are visible to inner modules, and invisible to modules at the same or outer levels. On the one hand, we want to reduce automatic visibility to inner modules, and on the other hand we would like to extend it to outer modules. What usually happens here is that the owner module identifies which objects should be seen, and it is up to the user modules to request visibility. The visibility may be identified implicitly or explicitly. Identifying the visible objects takes three forms.

1. *Separation of the interface and implementation*. The objects that should be available are listed in the interface, and all others are hidden in the implementation part (e.g. Ada). A user module requests access to all or some of the objects by using the module name (Figure 7.6).
2. *Explicit inner scope*. Some languages grant no visibility to inner scope (e.g. Euclid). Then visibility of selected objects is made available to inner modules by means of the pervasive clause, which grants read-only access, or by an immediately inner module *importing* the object in read-only or read-write mode. In addition, all the objects of an entire module may be imported using the module name. Granting inner scope is merely a special case of granting outer scope.
3. *Explicit outer scope*. All objects to be made available must be listed in an *export* list. They are then acquired individually through *import* lists in the user modules (e.g. Euclid, Modula-2, Gypsy, CHILL). Figure 7.7 illustrates this approach.

Let us compare these methods. Firstly, for *ease of use*, the interface implementation method is better as it concentrates on the module level and gives a clear grouping of data. Having explicit scoping is, on the other hand, more powerful, but can become messy when importing is done, variable by variable, at the routine level. Secondly, *control* of what is accessed in the first method is entirely vested in the owner, but then all users may take advantage. It is interesting that only one language, Gypsy [Ambler *et al.*, 1977], extends the idea of explicit scope control to include a specification by the owner as to which user modules are permitted to import, with the default being all. Although it seems the ultimate in control, this addition is contrary to large programming project methodology, where modules are developed separately, often without direct knowledge of the names of other

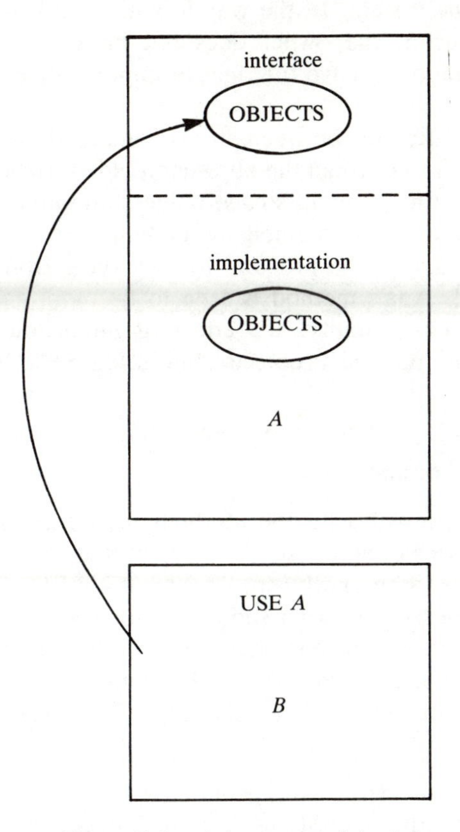

Figure 7.6 Access control in Ada

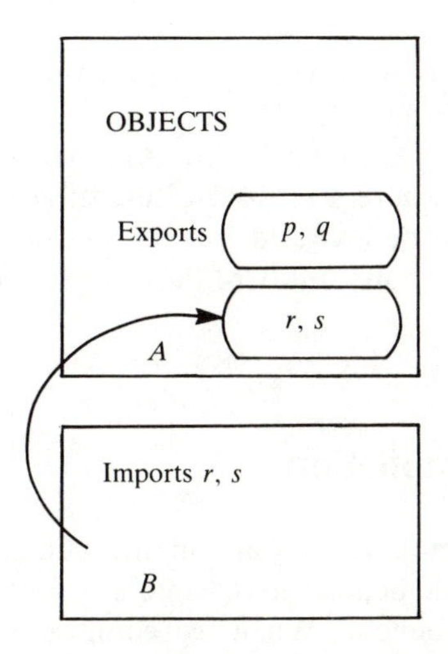

Figure 7.7 Access control in Euclid

modules in the same system. In the way in which explicit inner scoping is implemented in Euclid, the owner does not have complete control: all immediately inner modules have the right to import objects and to pass this right on.

The essential difference between the two methods is that in Ada the default is to import (i.e. USE) all the objects provided in the owner module's interface, whereas with export lists each object is treated individually. This individual treatment can lead to ambiguity in names from different modules, although Modula-2 avoids the problem by specifying from whence objects are to be imported. Ada's method is seen to be more general because in addition to the group visibility, the effect of import/output lists can be obtained by taking individual objects and using RENAMES in the user module.

Control of the kind of access

Earlier languages such as Euclid and Modula-2 concentrate on read-only or read-write as the levels of access that can be granted for objects. In both of these languages, it is the user who specifies what kind of access is required, rather than the owner saying what should be allowed.

In Ada, the owner is in complete control and the kind of access is specified with the type, not the object. By default, users can create and access objects in any manner valid for that type. The owner can then restrict this access in two ways:

- PRIVATE – The user may create, assign and test objects of the type, but may not use any other operations (e.g. arithmetic, I/O) unless these are supplied by the owner as valid for the type.
- LIMITED PRIVATE – as for PRIVATE except that assignment and testing are disallowed.

In other words, objects of private types may only be manipulated in ways specified by the owner module. There is a good discussion on when private types should be used in Gardner [1984]. Another level of restriction is that provided by CHILL, where a FORBID clause attached to a record indicates that the fields may not be accessed. As yet there is not much experience in this area, and the power and utility of these approaches will become evident as time goes by.

7.4 Separate compilation

We have discussed modules before, in the context of the separation of specification and implementation (Chapters 2 and 4); their use in access control is an added benefit. When we come actually to use modules in system building, we find a third advantage – that of efficiency during the development phase. In a nutshell, modules are self-contained, and can therefore be compiled as separate entities and stored away in libraries for later use. Programs that use a particular module need only have access to the specification part (which encapsulates all that the program is permitted to see), so that during compilation only this part is passed through the compiler. The compiler is able to check that all uses of the objects available through the module are correct, and has all the information necessary to generate code for such uses. Once the compilation is successful, the linker takes over and brings in the implementation parts of the modules, linking them together to form an executable program. This is a very powerful technique, but it brings with it its own problems in terms of *compilation*, *recompilation* and *language design*.

Compilation

The provision of modules and their use in access control has changed the face of compilation methods. A simple stack mechanism no longer mirrors the name spaces, and new symbol organizations are needed. A thorough study of a workable method is given in Cook and LeBlanc [1983]. In essence, the symbol table is a free list of entries with no implied scope or visibility. Instead each entry carries with it an explicit indication of these properties.

One of the biggest problems that advocates of modularity – and hence separate compilation – had to overcome was that in some cases the cost of development went up, not down as was expected. The reason is that, in a modular system, uses of objects are declared and then checked for consistency. This takes time, compared to the old monolithic model where all objects were automatically available. Moreover, there is an age-old tendency to guard against any eventuality which leads programmers to the habit of exporting and importing more than they actually need – just in case. The resulting explosion of the symbol table makes a significant increase in compilation speed and space. For example, in a private study of an industrial company using access control across 1500 modules, it was found that each module used on average 22 other modules. This meant opening 22 files and reading their interfaces, resulting in close on 3000 symbol table entries taking up 256 Kbytes.

Reducing compilation cost can therefore be seen as primarily a managerial problem – programmers must be educated into confining their use lists to those objects that are actually needed. Various technical improvements can be made, though, including ultra-efficient file handling during compilation (not usual under most operating systems) and the flagging on import lists of those identifiers that are actually used in the module [Kamel and Gammage, 1986].

Recompilation

A consequence of separate compilation of modules is that a library management system can initiate the automatic recompilation of modules that are affected by a module lower down the usage path being altered. In other words, if module X is altered, then all modules M_i that use module X are affected. The effect is at two levels: if a change is made to the specification of X then all the M_i must be recompiled, but, if only the implementation is altered, the actual compiled code of the M_i is unaffected and only relinking is required.

This process can have a cumulative effect, known as 'trickle down compilation'. If a change in X causes the M_i to be recompiled, the system must examine which modules use each of the M_i and initiate further recompilations if necessary. The cost of such recompilations can be horrendous, and studies have been made of how to keep them under control. Dausmann [1986] describes a system designed to decrease the set of necessary recompilations by basing the analysis of effect on a finer grain of information than the broad compilation units. Given Figure 7.8, the question is: if P3 is recompiled, should P4 be recompiled?

Looking at the example carefully, we see the connection between P2 and P3 is based on the type *t* which is used in the definition of type *dt*. Since P4 does not refer to *dt*, a change in P3 cannot affect P4. Using Dausmann's system, P4 would not be recompiled.

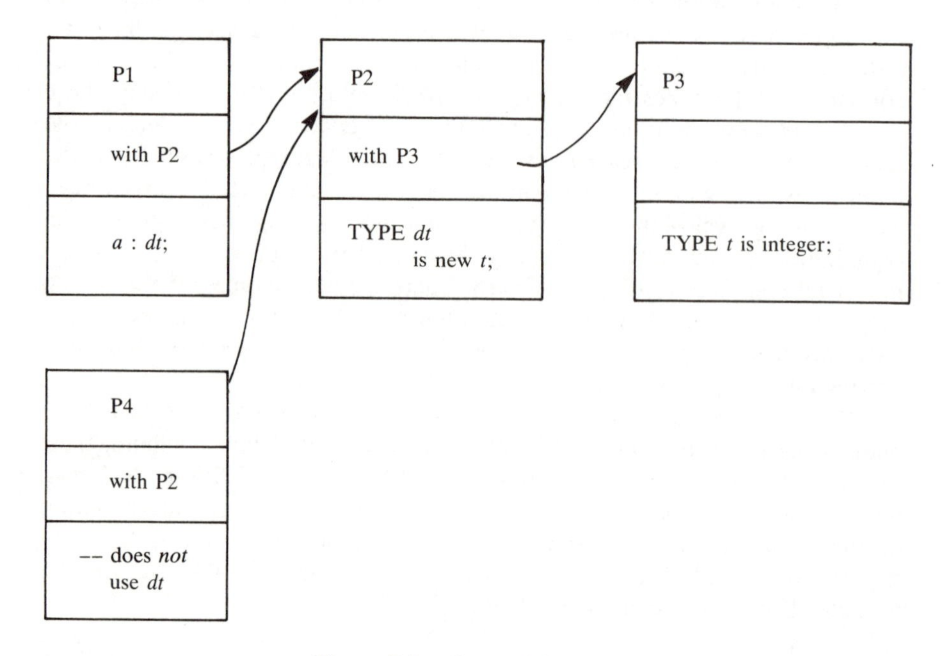

Figure 7.8 Some Ada units

Effect on language design

Dausmann [1986] points out that the necessary name analysis required to support reduced compilation is a complex semantic task for an Ada compiler. The main causes are overloading and the indirect naming permitted through USE clauses. From this point of view, module-based import mechanisms (like Ada's) are unattractive, and the entity-based mechanisms of CHILL and Modula-2 are preferable. Ada can easily be restricted to entity-based importing by simply avoiding the USE clause. The WITH clause gives access to a required module, and objects can then either be given their full names using dot notation or, if this tedious, RENAMES can be used to provide a shorter, local name. There is evidence that software houses are beginning to follow this route for the increase in compilation efficiency, but also because indirect names are deemed to hinder the understandability of a module.

7.5 Exception handling

The other side of the coin for data protection is program protection; in other words, protecting the normal execution of the program from being disturbed by bad data or data that arrives unexpectedly. This aspect of programming is particularly relevant in real-time systems where it is essential that the program be able to react to outside stimuli speedily and without danger of crashing. The unpredictable nature of such stimuli renders the normal sequential programming constructs inadequate, and we need to provide a separate construct which is activated in a different way. The usual name for such a construct is an *exception handler*. However, as Ghezzi and Jazayeri [1982] point out:

> The concept of an exception condition can hardly be stated in absolute terms. Programs are often required to behave reasonably under a wide range of circumstances, even in the presence of failure of the underlying hardware/software supports, or of events that happen so infrequently as to be considered anomalous, or of invalid input data. However, what is considered to be a normal processing state is a design decision taken by the designer, and it depends on the nature of the application. As a consequence, an anomalous processing state (or exception) does not necessarily mean that we are in the presence of a catastrophic error, but rather that the unit executing is unable to proceed in a manner that leads to normal termination.

A more apt name for the construct would therefore be an *implicitly called unit*, but the term 'exception' has stuck.

In an early paper, Goodenough [1975] traces the history of languages with some sort of exception handling features and outlines a notation for a generalized construct. In applying his ideas to other languages, three issues are continually raised, i.e.

- should control flow after an exception imply the resumption or termination of the module?
- should the handler be associated statically or dynamically with the place where the exception occurs?
- should exception handlers be placed conspicuously in the program or hidden away?

These language issues are now dealt with in turn.

Control flow

The issue that makes the biggest impact on the power and flexibility of an exception mechanism is where control flows after an exception has been dealt with. The first school supports normal structured programming in that it opts for the familiar procedure call mechanism, with control returning to the point where the exception occurred, i.e. a *resumption* model (Figure 7.9a). This view is adopted by PL/1, Mesa and Algol 68's error procedures for its transput system. The alternative approach is known as the *termination* model (Figure 7.9b). Here, the exception handler forms a block of code which in effect replaces the part of the program that would have been executed in the event of no exception being raised. Consequently, the module that was executing will be exited and an explicit re-call of it will have to be made for it to resume. Ada and CLU adopt this solution. CHILL, depending on what the exception handler is appended to, allows both concepts.

Critics of current implementations maintain that following one of the two models is inadequate. Given that there are several alternative courses of action when an exception is raised (e.g. abandon, retry, repair), they argue that separate constructs must be provided to distinguish between these possibilities, and in so doing increase clarity and understanding. Goodenough [1975] states that there is a 'need for a less rigid notation so that exceptions raised by different operations can be potentially implemented differently depending on their expected frequency and type of use'.

Supporters of the termination model claim that either the occasions when a program needs to resume execution immediately after the detection of an exception are too rare to be justified [Liskov and Snyder, 1979] or it is possible to simulate resumption given restricted syntactic tools. This must be weighed against the contrary view that these cases are too important to be disregarded.

The greater complexity of the resumption model can be seen in the interrelationship between the procedure that contains the exception handling code and the procedure that raises the exception. In the termination model, the normal one-way master-slave dependency of a calling procedure on the called procedure is upheld, and the follow-up action is the straightforward task of deleting the activation record of the caller. In the resumption model, both parties have to establish a more

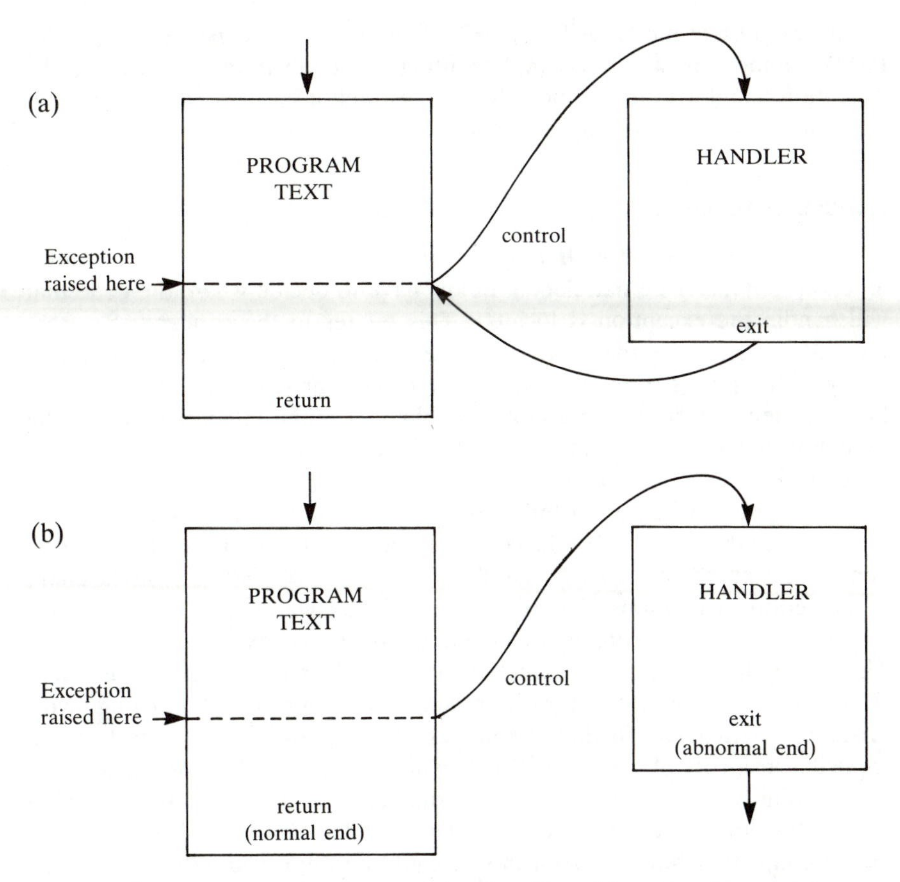

Figure 7.9 Models for exception handling: (a) resumption model; (b) termination model

involved two-way mapping, i.e. mutual dependency exists. Furthermore, the description of this mutual dependency for possibly more than one of the various types of exception calls complicates the procedure's interface requirements.

It can be argued that the resemblance of the resumption model to a normal procedure call mechanism is an advantage since it does not clash with the regular rules of structured programming, but the extra complications involved with exceptions weaken this connection. Termination is more likely to satisfy the goals of robustness and coherency, since it lends itself to the more regular and natural idea of a collection of exit points from a procedure, divided into those of a normal *return* and those of an abnormal *exit*.

Finally, termination has the advantage that it supports abstraction by means of a model of software consisting of multiple levels of abstraction with each abstract operation always terminating (albeit sometimes by signalling an exception). In contrast, this idea seems to have been confused in the resumption model as Lee [1983] elaborates: 'The concept of a (lower-level) component which is implementing some abstraction invoking the exception handler in the higher-level of abstraction in order to complete its operations as in the resumption model, does not seem appropriate'.

Handler association

The previous issue dealt with *how* the control of a program should flow after an exception has been handled. We now have to decide *where* the code that will handle the exception is located. This relates to the concept of a non-local GOTO, a feature that challenged the pillars of structured programming. Many of the points of view on this issue revolve around how modern ideas have refined this primitive concept so that the environment in which the exception is handled is made more or less compatible with the state of the program in which the exception is raised.

The issue is whether to bind exception handlers to procedures at run-time or require them to be declared and bound at compile-time. The first approach is known as *dynamic* handler association, where the dynamic chain of procedure activations is implicitly traced backwards until an exception handler whose label matches the name of the raised exception is reached. This policy has been implemented in varying degrees by PL/1, Mesa and Ada. The other approach, known as *static* association, has the analogy with procedure parameters in that the names of exceptions have to be declared explicitly in a sort of 'export list' that will give some indication of how the two disjoint blocks of code should be connected. CLU and CHILL roughly follow this direction while Cocco and Dulli [1982], Knudsen [1984] and Lee [1983] conjecture how the Ada model could be improved with a few static specifications.

Irrespective of which approach is taken, two important provisos for exceptions are that they should correspond to subprograms that are *called in the environment of the caller* and that they must be *visible* to the routines that raise them. With such precautions, the dynamic scope rule can prove to have the edge over the static mechanism. As MacLennan [1983] states: 'It is often the case that different callers of a subprogram will want to handle exceptions arising from that subprogram in different ways. If the handler for an exception were bound in a subprogram's environment of definition, it would be fixed for all time. In that case, it might as well be made part of the subprogram.' A very good example of how different handlers can be provided is given in the Ada manual page 11–6 [Department of Defense, 1983].

This policy is fine, except that a safe dynamic construct has proven difficult to implement. PL/1's ON conditions are fraught with possibilities for side-effects and misunderstandings [Ghezzi and Jazayeri, 1982], and even Ada is not free from criticism. The debate about Ada centres on the degree to which the raising of an exception can propagate back through its nested activation levels. Unlike PL/1, there is some control in anticipating which handler may be justified because an exception handler can only be attached to the end of a procedure body, package body or block, after the keyword EXCEPTION. Thus the way in which the exception handler is found is not as convoluted as in PL/1. A handler in a particular block is forbidden to override another handler for the same exception; in fact, the occlusion of an exception handler can only be done by a new one being declared in an inner block. Hence, if a particular unit does not provide a handler for a certain exception, control will pass to the end of the unit and it will terminate. All the statements between the point at which the exception was raised and the EXCEPTION WHEN clause will be skipped over, the exception will be implicitly re-raised at the beginning of its enclosed unit, and will repeatedly raise itself in a straightforward (unlike PL/1) linearly recursive manner.

However, fault is still found with this unrestricted propagation. Although the PL/1 problems have been alleviated, the possibility of ambiguous effects resulting from an exception being activated at different points in the program has not been eradicated. Cocco and Dulli [1982] and Lee [1983] suggest identical solutions. They campaign for separate constructs that recognize that there are two different levels at which an exception can be handled. There are those exceptions that should be handled locally (within the unit that raised the exception) and those for which it must be explicitly stated that they will be propagated externally to their enclosing unit. As in Ada, a unit which cannot handle an exception must be terminated and the exception re-raised elsewhere in a unit that either statically encloses or calls the previous one. This fits in nicely with MacLennan's observations and adds that touch of safety lacking in an unrestrained mechanism.

This approach seems to be implemented in CHILL which lists in the procedure heading the names of those exceptions that will not be handled locally. CLU does this as well, but does not allow the propagation to extend past the level of a procedure's immediate caller without having to be explicitly re-raised. CLU, unlike most other implementations, is a single-level mechanism (as opposed to Ada which is multi-level) and it also does not allow the unit that raised an exception to handle it.

Both the Lee [1983] and Liskov and Snyder [1979] papers justify their policies by falling back on arguments for methodical programming. The specification of the interface to a unit needs only to specify the exceptions associated with that interface, since the caller of a procedure only wants to execute its 'abstract action' and does not and should not need to know about its internal workings. Only those exceptions that a procedure may cause to be raised externally must be visible since they form part of the abstract behaviour of the procedure.

Handler placement

Exception handling is not an easy or conventional area of programming, and the language can play an important part in increasing the reliability and maintainability of a system. This raises the question of whether the visual appearance of the error processing sections within a block of program code is conspicuous enough. Redwine [1981] argues that the traditional conceptualization of a software procedure (i.e. that it has the structure of a dominating constructive purpose, with any error processing being pushed to the background) is a misguided one that does not encourage good programming style.

He found that the bulk of code written for certain types of software (business application systems, economic and social research) using input from human beings (and other error-prone sources) does not deal with the so-called primary constructive purpose of a procedure. Hence he states a quite valid case for a construct that allows the exception handling routines – which are in the majority – a more prominent position in the layout of the procedure. His new paradigm would raise the exception handlers to parity with the main function in a visibly explicit manner. A procedure would be visibly partitioned into the two functions by a *defence line*, which corresponds to WHEN clauses listing the exceptions that could be raised. Now, since all the error conditions are forced into the second half of the procedure, one can see more clearly what the primary function has to do.

Existing implementations, even in the newer languages, do not go as far as Redwine's suggestions. In CLU and CHILL, handlers are added on to the end of the statement, procedure definition or process definition from which the raising of an exception could emanate, and in Ada they can be placed at the end of a block, which effectively means anything longer than an expression. However, by confining exception handlers to the end of compilation units – subprograms, packages or tasks – one can achieve in Ada the separation promoted by Redwine. Thus the whole development process is simplified. All the exceptions that could occur must now be rigorously and explicitly specified and brought together, rather than being distributed piecemeal around. As Cocco and Dull [1982] observe, by associating exceptions and exception handlers with units, we are following a design style based on the recognition of abstraction.

Examples of the use of exceptions are given in Ada at the end of Section 4.3.

Exercises

1. Discuss the key issues identified by Ambler and Hoch [1977] in their study of the protection provided by current languages. Illustrate your answer with reference to the languages you have studied, giving brief examples where necessary. Mention whether the facilities you describe were intended to be used for the purpose of protection.
2. Programming languages support a variety of protection mechanisms. Discuss these mechanisms with reference to Pascal, Modula-2 and Ada,

giving short explanatory examples. Mention to what extent the protection can be unilateral and whether cooperation is required.

3. There is a growing move away from unit-based import mechanisms towards entity-based import mechanisms. Describe the two techniques, with examples from existing languages, and discuss the effect of such a move on both programmer and compiler efficiency.
4. The watershed for different exception mechanisms is whether they support the termination or the resumption model for control flow. Describe these with reference to existing languages, and discuss how the approach taken on this aspect influences the handler association and handler placement mechanisms of a language.

References

Ambler, A.L. and Hoch, C.G., 1977. 'A study of protection in programming languages', Proceedings of the Conference on Language Design for Reliable Software. In *SIGPLAN*, **12(3)**, 25–40.

Ambler, A.L., Good, D.I., Browne, J.C., Burger, W.F., Cohen, R.M., Hoch, C.G. and Wells, R.E., 1977. 'GYPSY: a language for specification and implementation of verifiable programs', Proceedings of the Conference on Language Design for Reliable Software. In *SIGPLAN*, **12(3)**, 1–10.

Bishop, J.M. and Barron, D.W., 1980. 'Procedure calling and structured architectures', *Computer Journal*, **23**, 115–123.

Boute, R.T. and Jackson, M.I., 1981. 'A joint evaluation of the programming languages Ada and CHILL', Proceedings of the 4th International Conference on Software Engineering for Telecommunication Switching Systems, Coventry, UK, July 1981, pp. 20–24.

Cocco, N. and Dulli, S., 1982. 'A mechanism for exception handling and its verification rules', *Computer Languages*, **7(2)**, 89–102.

Cook, R.P. and LeBlanc, T.J., 1983. 'A symbol table abstraction to implement languages with explicit scope control', *IEEE-SE*, **9(1)**, 8–12.

Dausmann, M., 1986. 'Reducing compilation costs for software systems in Ada', Proceedings of the IFIP WG2.4 Symposium on *Systems Implementation Languages – Experience and Assessment*, Canterbury, September 1984, Amsterdam, North-Holland, in press.

Department of Defense, 1983. *Military Standard for the Ada Programming Language*, MIL-STD-1815A.

Gardner, M.R., 1984. 'When to use private types', *Ada Letters*, **III(6)**, 66–78.

Ghezzi, C. and Jazayeri, M., 1982. *Programming Language Concepts*, New York, Wiley.

Goodenough, J.B., 1975. 'Exception handling: issues and a proposed notation', *CACM*, **18(12)**, 683–696.

Johnston, J.B., 1971. 'The contour model of block structured processes', *SIGPLAN*, **6(2)**, 55–82.

Kamel, R.F. and Gammage, N.D., 1986. 'Further experience with separate compilation at BNR', Proceedings of the IFIP WG2.4 Symposium on *Systems Implementation Languages – Experience and Assessment*, Canterbury, September 1984, Amsterdam, North-Holland, in press.

Knudsen, J.L., 1984. 'Exception handling – a static approach', *SPE*, **14(5)**, 429–449.

Lee, P.A., 1983. 'Exception handling in C programs', *SPE*, **13(5)**, 389–406.

Liskov, B.H. and Snyder, A., 1979. 'Exception handling in CLU', *IEEE-SE*, **5(6)**, 546–558.

MacLennan, B.J., 1983. *Principles of Programming Languages: Design, Evaluation and Implementation*, Holt, Rinehart and Winston.

Organick, E.I., 1973. *Computer Systems Organization – the B5700/B6700 Series*, New York, Academic Press.

Redwine, S.T. Jr, 1981. 'A paradigm for dealing with exceptions', *SIGPLAN Notices*, **16(5)**, 36–38.

Welsh, J., Sneeringer, M.J. and Hoare, C.A.R., 1977. 'Ambiguities and insecurities in Pascal', *SPE*, **7(6)**, 685–696.

Chapter 8 The Way Ahead

Data abstraction is now firmly entrenched in programming language design and methodology. What of the future? What problem areas remain and what new directions are possible?

8.1 The status quo

In the broad area of general-purpose programming languages, the Pascal mould has become a near standard. There is general acceptance of such fundamental structures as procedures and functions, value and var parameter passing, if–then–else, while–do, case subranges, enumerations, arrays, records and pointers. Together these can form a considerable part of the basis for any new language, as they did for Ada. At the time of Ada's definition, further concepts were gaining credence, namely strong typing, modularity and information hiding. It is probable that future languages with the same goals as Ada will look much the same. However, certain problem spots remain.

8.2 On-going development

The most important area for concern with data abstraction is the position of languages in the whole programming effort. Specifically, one is looking at

- formal specification,
- verification,
- system design,
- programming environments.

Specifications were discussed fully in Chapter 3. The problem seems to be both one of notation – it should be possible to make these more readable – and of approach. Does one come in with an idea of how a program should operate and describe this, or does one step back and model the functions in an abstract way? Constructive specifications are perhaps easier to formulate, but may be less effective than the modelled (definitional) ones. Attempts are being made to define specification languages, and to use these to fix the semantics of the programming language itself, but nothing has yet achieved practical significance. As was explained in Chapter 3, a suitable specification language is a *sine qua non* for effective verification. Nevertheless, techniques for verification can still be developed, and these are leading to the exciting area of program synthesis.

Although this book gives a full account of what data abstraction is and how it is integrated into programming languages, it does not discuss how abstraction is really used at the system level. How does the decomposition process proceed? On what basis does one decide to group procedures or form new types or set up new processes? Moreover, how does one describe the resulting design? The language itself is really at too low a level. An excellent starting point for further study here is the book by Buhr [1984], which describes both a design methodology using Ada and a graphical notation for illustrating the design.

The place of a language in its environment is often overlooked by language specialists, and even when it is addressed there is a great variation in the results. It is generally believed that the success of three of the most widely used languages, i.e. BASIC, UCSD Pascal and C (with UNIX), is largely due to the powerful yet simple environments in which they are embedded. When Ada was mooted, a simultaneous project was initiated to define an APSE (Ada Programming Support Environment). Little has come of this, and Ada compilers in use today use the operating systems and software of their host machines. Perhaps it is intrinsically more difficult to embed a language system in a large mainframe computer than in a single-user micro or small minicomputer, but this problem definitely needs to be solved. The current research was presented at an ACM conference in April 1984 [SIGPLAN, 1984], but much of the work is directed towards specific projects, rather than any underlying principles.

8.3 Remaining problems

At a working conference organized by IFIP WG2.4 (Systems implementation languages) in September 1984, the question was raised as to what had been achieved and where we should be going. To sum up the answers, someone wrote up the statement

SILs are solved.

meaning that there is no further work to be done. The audience did not agree, and modified the statement thus:

SEQUENTIAL SILs for VON NEUMANN ARCHITECTURES are solved.

This highlights the two major areas of concern that have not yet been fully covered by data abstraction. Firstly, we need to know a lot more about concurrency, how and why it operates and how best to use it. Equally, the languages features have not yet stabilized and there is a need for some unifying theory. Secondly, there is a whole new generation of computers in the making and they are not all going to follow the classic sequential model. Language designers need to be aware of these trends, and it is not sufficient simply to leave the innovations to those who promote the new breeds of functional and logical languages. Particularly in the realm of protection, the computer architects are going to start leading the way, providing facilities that may well alter the way in which we describe modules and access control at the moment.

Concurrency and protection are two big areas of concern. There are also two smaller, but definitely important, aspects which need attention. As pointed out in Chapter 2, input/output has not kept pace with the development of modern languages. While it is fashionable to use data abstraction to delegate input/output to a set of procedures, there is some doubt as to whether this is indeed the best way. Maybe input/output is such a fundamental requirement that it needs to be integrated into the language at the statement level. The other problem area is loops, as fully discussed in Chapter 5. Here, a possible direction is the extension of generic packaging facilities to make them able to cope with iterators and generators.

8.4 New directions

One of the most exciting proposals for a new direction was made by Shaw and Wulf [1980] when they suggested applying data abstraction to programming language design. Looking at languages from a distance, they saw that language designers tend to make pre-emptive decisions about the representation of features. These decisions are based on broad experience and are usually beneficial, but can be detrimental to program clarity, structure and efficiency. For example, they cite the usual representation of arrays as contiguous elements in row order. Why should they not be stored as sparse arrays or with linked storage? When programmers learn of the representation, and find it is not efficient for their purposes, they bypass the natural approach to a solution by introducing tricks such as storing two arrays in one, or not passing arrays as parameters when they should.

Pre-emptive decisions conflict with the fundamental precept of structured programming that the *order* of design decisions is crucial. One should first make the decisions that are least likely to change, and then those that may well change. In today's languages, decisions about storage allocation, dynamic variables, loop control exceptions and even operators are already made, yet they could change with specific use. Such pre-emptives introduce circumlocutions, prevent optimizations and encourage low level programming.

Shaw and Wulf propose that we should distinguish between the essential semantics of a feature and its incidental semantics. We can then use data abstraction to separate:

> the specification of a language, which gives its essential semantics and functional properties (the 'what')

from

> a variety of implementations which can be verified to conform to the specification (the 'how').

Thus a language would be supplied with:

- a syntax
- incomplete semantics
- essential properties of remaining semantics
- useful defaults for incomplete constructs

and there would be a flexible facility which would

1. reduce distributed effects to a small set of events,
2. delineate effects that must take place and the permited variability,
3. give the programmer control over the points of variability.

In such a way, data abstraction can prove itself to be the cornerstone for language design, as well as for programming.

References

Buhr, R.J.A., 1984. *System Design with Ada*, New Jersey, Prentice-Hall.

Shaw, M. and Wulf, W.A., 1980. 'Toward relaxing assumptions in languages and their implementations', *SIGPLAN*, **15(3)**, 45–61.

SIGPLAN, 1984. Proceedings of the Symposium on Practical Software Development Environments, *SIGPLAN*, **19(5)** (also as *Software Engineering Notes*, **9(3)**, 1984).

Data Abstraction Self-Study Topics

Objectives

- to conduct a thorough literature survey on a given topic;
- to find two or three important points of controversy or discussion on that topic;
- to present in an organized way the relative points of view;
- to assess and evaluate them, and to come to some conclusions.

Topics and key references

1. **Enumerated types**

   Harland, D.M. and Gunn, H.I.E., 1983. 'Another look at enumerated types', *SIGPLAN*, **17(7)**, 62–71.

   Moffat, D.V., 1983. 'Enumerated types in Pascal, Ada and beyond', *SIGPLAN*, **16(2)**, 77–82.

2. **Exceptions**

   Ichbiah, J., Heliard, J.C., Roubine, O., Barnes, J.G.P., Krieg-Bruckner, B. and Wichmann, B.A., 1979. 'Exception handling in *Rationale for Ada*', *SIGPLAN*, **14(6)**, 12.

   Redwine, S.J., 1981. 'A paradigm for dealing with exceptions', *SIGPLAN*, **16(5)**, 36–38.

3. **Type equivalence and checking**

   Rowe, L.A., 1981. 'Types workshop', *SIGPLAN*, **16(1)**, 43–52.

   Welsh, J., Sneeringer, M.J. and Hoare, C.A.R., 1977. 'Ambiguities and insecurities in Pascal', *SPE*, **7(6)**, 685–696.

4. **Real types**

   Ichbiah, J., Heliard, J.C., Roubine, O., Barnes, J.G.P., Krieg-Bruckner, B. and Wichmann, B.A., 1979. 'Numeric types in *Rationale for Ada*', *SIGPLAN*, **14(6)**, 5.1–5.17.

   Fisher, G., 1984. 'Universal arithmetic packages', *Ada Leters*, **III(6)**, 30–47.

5. **Access types**

   Ichbiah, J., Heliard, J.C., Roubine, O., Barnes, J.G.P., Krieg-Bruckner, B. and Wichmann, B.A., 1979. 'Access types in

Rationale for Ada', *SIGPLAN*, **14(6)**, 6.1–6.12.

Price, A.M., 1984. 'Defining dynamic variables and abstract data types in Pascal', *SIGPLAN*, **19(2)**, 85–91.

6. **Block structure**

Tennent, R.D., 1982. 'Two examples of block structuring', *SPE*, **12**, 385–392.

Clark, L.A., Wileden, J.C. and Wolf, A.L., 1980. 'Nesting in Ada is for the birds', *SIGPLAN*, **15(11)**, 139–145.

Notes

1. The references given are mostly dated prior to mid-1983. You should check subsequent journals.
2. Don't concentrate only on Ada and Pascal – try to bring in other languages, even the older ones.
3. Beware of duplicating verbatim the arguments and organization given in the references.

Index